Revealing the Heart of a Man
What Men Wish Women Knew

D. Jackson

Revealing the Heart of a Man…What Men Wish Women
Knew
Published by D. Jackson
Copyright© 2015

ISBN 9781505320312

Scripture quotations are from The *King James Version of the
Bible and the Revised Standard Version of the Bible.*

This book is dedicated to

my most favorite person in the entire world,

my daughter,

Nayonna Murchison

I adore you with all my heart!

It is also dedicated to

my best friend,

Gerald Jackson

Thank you for your invaluable input and support, and

for **making a difference in my life!**

CONTENTS

To the wonderful men who so graciously consented to be interviewed:

I could never thank you enough for your rich contributions to this book. Many of you have expressed how these interviews were cathartic and that you considered this book to be a proper venue to lend credence to your voices. I only hope it does justice to the warm and sensitive spirit in which you responded with your insights, wisdoms, and reflections. They will certainly prove monumental in repairing and bridging the gap which exist in many relationships today.

Please never forget that somewhere, someone, or an entire relationship is strengthened and encouraged by wisdoms you shared or advice you gave. Always remember that you have been a marvelous tool in the hands of God; a tool that brings healing and restoration to one of His most treasured creations: the male-female relationship.

I honor you-for honoring me with your heart. I can't wait for the *fruit of its revelation!*

INTRODUCTION

Revealing the Heart of a Man...What Men Wish Women Knew was written to provide a safe venue for men to express their thoughts concerning women and relationships. I wanted men to have the liberty of saying--without hesitation or reservation--what they wish women knew!

Their perspectives do not come from the usual sources: the self-help gurus, syndicated relationship experts, talk show hosts, or others who crowd today's media. Instead, I purposely solicited the input of average males who could provide a detailed account and comprehensive insight into the female psyche, conduct, and character; based on knowledge derived from their everyday interactions and experiences with common issues that plague relationships.

The men had no prior knowledge of, or preparation for, the questions posed to them. I didn't want them to respond with any consideration of what they thought women would want to hear, or what I, as a female interviewer, expected them to say. Each interview session was taped, therefore, they are the verbatim transcribed responses from their hearts. No one man spoke as an authority on women, nor suggested what he shared applied to all women. Each one simply shared of his own experiences or personal observations.

The men were selected because of the positive vibe and warm aura they projected. I wanted to make certain from the outset the interviews would not become female-bashing sessions. They are representative of various ages, ethnicities, occupations, religious persuasions, cultural backgrounds, and geographical locations. Their ages range from 21 to 70. They are entrepreneurs, business owners, educators, law enforcement officers, carpenters, barbers, salesmen, military personnel, religious leaders, community activists, musicians, models, electricians, child advocates, artists, and psychologists.

Some names were purposely changed to protect the confidentiality of the men whose wives and significant others I know. Also, the ethnicities, ages, occupations, religious persuasions, and geographical locations were deliberately and strategically omitted, so the reader would not be prejudiced against or biased towards a particular demographic. Nor did I want the validity of their thoughts and feelings to be misplaced, discounted, negated, or lost to demographics. It is vitally important to me that the **emphasis and focus stay centered on the responses, perspectives, and points of views; as they reflect their sincere innermost thoughts and feelings and should be regarded and respected as such.**

My intent for this book is that it will accomplish several things:

First, it will defend against the prevailing myth that all men are the same and most are no good. I intend to dispel the myth that all men, in general, are:

A. Insensitive rather than sensitive

B. Careless rather than caring

C. Thoughtless rather than thoughtful

D. Inconsiderate rather than considerate

Secondly, this book will become a resource guide for married couples to refer to, to help them detect the challenges that come to marriages during trying times, and aid them in becoming stronger through the changing seasons of life.

Thirdly, the insights within each chapter would

challenge single men and women to properly discern where they are in their personal growth and development, and come to realize what they *really* want in a partner and a relationship.

Fourthly, this book will be used as a premarital aid to help engaged couples make the necessary adjustments, sooner rather than later, that would allow them to ward off potential conflicts that may prevent the impending marriage from reaching a true state of enjoyment and fulfillment.

Lastly, to my readers- **open your minds**-just as the men have **opened their hearts**- *because*, whether you are a man or a woman, there's so much truth in here for you, *it just might change your life!*

"I will praise you, for I am fearfully and wonderfully made."
Psalm 139:14

One: Her Endearing Qualities

The level of appreciation we have for a thing not only dictates the degree of importance we place on it, but it will also govern our actions and responses towards it. If there is a high level of regard or appreciation for a thing, then there is always a high level of care and maintenance given towards its preservation. On the other hand, if there is little regard or low appreciation for a thing, usually there are little or no real attempts made towards its preservation. In other words, the things we consider valuable or important to our lives are the things to which we give considerable time and effort. Left unattended to, very often, are those things we deem trivial or of little worth.

Considering these principles, I was motivated to ask the men to seriously reflect upon the endearing qualities of women. I was confident the affirming or reaffirming of such qualities would create in them a deeper appreciation of a woman's worth, and a greater awareness of her value.

I was even more confident their reflections would evoke in them a renewed and profound respect for the women in their lives, and inspire them to make new efforts and take more deliberate steps to increase the level of enjoyment and satisfaction within *their* personal relationships.

In another instance, my most sincere desire is that their responses would remind women of the endearing qualities that "real men" feel they uniquely possess, and concede with the men and the Word of God that they *are* indeed ***fearfully and wonderfully made!***

What endearing qualities do women possess?

Mamy: Women have the privilege and honor of bearing children for the continuation of the human race. They show great responsibility in keeping things together in the household. They are great organizers. Women are big influences on their offspring. The qualities of the kids are often a reflection of the time and care she invested in the rearing of them.

Dominic: Nurturing is one quality that stands out and that I see often. Women are great at nurturing children. When they are upset or down, they step right in and bring them back up to speed and get them back on track.

Arnold: Her ability to produce a child for her man. That's something that men will never understand. It's amazing how a woman will go through such pain and discomfort for such a long period of time. It's admirable that a woman is willing to subject herself to that.

Michael L.: I think women are naturally made better than men. They look better. They move better than men. They smell better than men and they feel better than men. They are softer, yet strong enough to carry a child and go through the labor of giving birth.

Tony D.: Women have a strong sense of motherhood and a strong sense of protection.

Travis: Women have great maternal instincts. They are very protective of any forces outside of the home that would attempt to threaten their family's safety.

Michael W.: Women are uniquely able to realize when the family is in trouble. Women were designed by God to discern when the family is in trouble and to what degree it is in trouble. They have more insight into the problems of the home because they look deeper into the ways of the household.

Gary: They are very skilled in running a household.

Lennie: Women possess so many positive qualities that are much underrated. The most positive quality is the ability to take care of a household. I don't think that we, as men, fully understand the dynamics of that position. To care for a household and all of its inhabitants takes a tremendous amount of mental and physical energy. Women give tremendous attention to caring for a household.

Timothy: Women are very intuitive to people's needs because they are natural nurturers. Women are the backbone of the country. They have persevered through all the tyranny and evil of men to support and raise families.

Michael L: Women think more multifaceted than men. With women, there is always more reasoning, nurturing, and a deeper understanding of issues. They may be less instinctive at the onset of everything, but as they go through everything, at the end of everything, they use their love and compassion to end an issue. They are more compassionate, nurturing, and go deeper into understanding and resolving issues than men.

Ryan: Women are nurturers. They seem to be

more open, in a lot of ways, about things.

Gilbert: Women have the ability to nurture. They are providers and good leaders. They have the ability to organize and the ability to think things through. They have a special gift of companionship and the gift of helping. They have the ability to bring people together. They have the ability to be peacemakers.

Robert B.: They are peacemakers and peacekeepers. They raise children. Women bring the power of love. If you look at a good family, you're looking at a powerful and wonderful mother. Women are dependable, nurturing, and forgiving. They are bright and insightful- kind of with an intuitive thing. They know things from the gut and they tend to be accurate in their knowing.

Carroll: Women have a better sense of intuition than men do. They are able to see through the stupidity of men. We need to listen to them more because of that. They are better grounded and are more in touch with the "stuff."

Kevin: Women have very keen senses. Their senses extend farther than men's do. Women can detect and see things that men can't and don't see.

Aaron: Women have the ability to be independent and handle their own. They know what they want and go for it. After they get where they want to be, they know what steps to take next. They can easily communicate to men what they want. They are intelligent and have good thought processes.

Larry: They are a nice complement to the man's thinking!

Malcolm: Women have a lot of positive energy, external and internal beauty, and a sincere enthusiasm for life!

Lawrence: Women have a strong sense of loyalty and faithfulness. They are very giving and loving.

Patrick: They are honest, caring, compassionate, and affectionate.

Sylvester: Women are strong and strong-minded. They possess a great sense of direction. As men, we sometimes tend to stray off course, but women seem to remain focused and aggressive in going after what they want or need.

Michael R: Women have purpose. They have great flexibility in making adjustments in situations that aren't what they appear to be. That flexibility allows them to take the steps necessary to turn negativity into positivity.

Bill: Women are compassionate, understanding, and have great flexibility and responsiveness.

Will: Friendship, openness, kindness, and friendliness are endearing qualities of women.

Roosevelt: There is a friendliness that a lot of women possess. They are very supportive. They seem to maintain a good sense of humor and outlook despite their situations. Women are naturally compassionate. Women are ambitious and are visionaries. They have great vision in pursuing their ambitions.

Jermaine H.: A lot of women are very confident in expressing themselves and their feelings. They are very giving of themselves. They have an emotional quality that is very positive, in a lot of aspects. They are positive influences.

Tony F.: Women are nurturing because of their maternal instincts. They are caring and compassionate individuals. Not only are those qualities innate, but they are transferable- meaning that those traits are transferred to their child, boyfriend, and friends. Women tend to see the beauty in most people and situations. They can respond to people and situations with care and compassion.

Gerald: It's great how women bring out the best in men. It's nothing in particular that they have to do. It's a natural thing. Men want to be better people when they have the right woman. They are nurturing and love unconditionally. Most men really need that unconditional love.

Christopher: Women possess the ability to make sound decisions. Women are consistent in supporting their men. Even in extreme situations, a woman will support her man in achieving his goals. I've come to realize that women really do assist men in reaching their full potential.

*"As a ring of gold in a swine's snout-- so is the
lovely woman who lacks discretion."*
Proverbs 11:22

Two: Her Undesirable Traits

At the conclusion of a very insightful and
delightful interview with Travis, I commented on how I
particularly appreciated the forthright and direct approach
he took with his responses. He humorously entered into
a friendly rebuttal. "But," he said, "Will the women really
want to hear what we have to say? Will they really listen?
Don't get me wrong. I appreciate what you're doing. I
think it's great, but some women can't handle how frank
or honest a man can be. They think when he's
straightforward, he is cold-hearted or insensitive. A lot of
women can't handle the straight truth as it comes from a
man. I don't want to discourage you and I wish you much
success in what you're trying to do- but will they listen to
what we have to say?" I simply responded- "Real women
will."

Real women are not threatened by the truth. As
hurtful and challenging as the truth may be, a real woman

respects it and adheres to its healing virtues. She will not become combative or confrontational. She will graciously concede to truth's validity and allow its higher standard to achieve a greater expansion of her and the relationship. A real woman wants to hear, learn, know, and understand what comprises her man. She is intrigued by his individuality and interested in every aspect of him; his personal aspirations, preferences, likes, and even dislikes. She is always willing to hear his heart and mind so that she can equip herself to become the help suitable in his quest to fulfill all that God has called him to be.

Therefore, I challenge the women. How will you handle their hearts and minds if you see yourself reflected in some of the views in this chapter, or when you realize that your man shares a common opinion? Will you use it against him as a point of contention to justify where you are? Or will you use it as a point of revelation to encourage you to do your part to rid the relationship of the idiosyncrasies that keep it from reaching its full potential?

You see, it is easy for us to concentrate on another's inadequacies and dismiss our own deficiencies, as suggested in **Matthew 7: 3-4:** [3] And why beholdest thou the mote that is in thy brother's eye, but considerest not the beam that is in thine own eye? [4] Or how wilt thou say to thy brother, Let me pull out the mote out of thine eye; and, behold, a beam is in thine own eye?

In explanation, as women, rarely do we have difficulty with expressing what we consider are the faults of men, but when the men try to voice their criticisms of us, oftentimes, we become guarded and defensive to the point of reasoning that our undesirable actions were precipitated by their undesirable behaviors. However, we should never excuse or justify less than desirable behaviors, actions, or reactions on our part. Nor can we any longer hold men accountable for our inadequacies or indiscretions. We are responsible for upholding and maintaining our own standard of morals and code of ethics.

Therefore, we must give earnest heed and careful attention to the concerns of our men and accept their constructive criticisms *as* well as their insights. Their mild correction and gentle rebuke is beneficial to helping us properly assess our own behavior, and holding us personally accountable to a higher standard of propriety.

What are undesirable traits in women?
Easily Given to Assumptions

Joseph: A lot of women are more given to assumptions. Many times their assumptions aren't based on facts, but a lack of trust.

Selfishness

Roosevelt: There are a lot of women who are not willing to share. It's so hard for them to compromise or sacrifice anything for the sake of the relationship.

Will: Some women say they want to compromise but they really don't. Compromising is one of the big things I try to do. You offer out the compromise and even though they say they wish to do the same, they don't really compromise.

Richard W.: Some women are not community-minded- as far as pitching in to help, no matter the cause.

Mike R.: A lot of women are self-centered. They tend to focus more on themselves than on others around them.

Malcolm: Some women are all about −"Me, me, me, me, me, me." I'll speak, "How you doing?" I will even hold a conversation with you. Afterwards, it's- "See you later, bye!" I would shy away from someone who thinks the world revolves around them and who is self-centered.

I can get along with anybody, but if you think it is all about you-- that's going to be a short relationship.

Timothy: Some women can be self-serving. It's all about giving to them or doing for them.

Chau: Some women can be very stubborn and never want to give in or compromise. Everything always has to be their way.

Bill: Some women have a sense of entitlement. They are selfish in that it's all about them. It's about what you're going to do for them.

Arrogance

Robert C.: Negative to me is a woman who is bourgeois. She is stuck on herself and feels that the whole world revolves around her. For instance, I don't need for you to keep telling me that you are a princess and need to be treated like a princess. You don't have to keep reminding me of that. I'm a man. I'll know how to treat you.

Gilbert: The most disturbing trait for me is when you speak to a woman- you're just being cordial- you're not trying to make a pass or come on to her but she responds like you're trying to hit on her. That's a turn-off. I'm giving her the respect that a queen should have but she gives me a response that is not of a queen.

Trevor: One thing that frustrates me is- I'm used to speaking to women and some of them don't speak back. It doesn't mean that I am trying to talk to you. I'm just saying hello in passing. Give me the courtesy of saying hello back. You can tell by the way that I said hello that I am not trying to date you. I'm just trying to be polite.

Overly Aggressive

Tony D.: Some women are too bossy and domineering, causing them to exhibit a lack of respect for men.

Kevin: Very negative to me is an overbearing woman.

Gerald: It is very negative to see an overly aggressive woman who feels as if she always has to be in control.

Richard C.: An overly aggressive woman is very negative to me.

Duncan: Some women come on too strong. That's a turn-off. To me, you don't have to do that to get close to someone. When they try too hard and come on too strong, it is a turn-off.

Too Smothering

Ty: I tell women who had friends before I ever knew them to not cut off their friends when we start getting tight. You shouldn't just cut off your friends. I won't cut mine out for you. When they call and want to go out, I'm gone. It's not that me and my friends go out all the time, but when they call, I'm out. A lot of women start cutting their friends off. They stop going out, stop calling and seeing them, and then expect to always be stuck up under you. "Operation Pressure"-they want to lock you down.

Daryl: Sometimes women are too controlling or needy. It can get to a point where the man may have a lot of friends but she expects him to spend less and less time with them and more and more time with her. She tries to get him to cut off everyone and everything at once. That's a little extreme.

Will: Some women can be a little aggressive in trying to engage your entire social life. They sometimes want to spend every free moment with you. It can be a little overwhelming. You shouldn't have to spend 100 percent of your time together. Some women want to spend every single second with you. It can be a little overbearing.

Overly Emotional

Joseph: At times, women don't listen. They get side-tracked by their emotions too easily. Instead of listening, they run off with their emotions before they have all the facts together or before they hear you out on a subject.

Reuben: This may be too stereotypical but they're too emotional at times. They're too emotional over situations that don't need to have too much emotion put into them. In some cases, their emotions make them too sheltering of children, sometimes it's to the point of the child's detriment.

Kevin: Women can be overly emotional at times. Men are moved by what they see and women are moved by what they feel. A lot of times, their emotions override them. There are some women who can't control their emotions. For instance, if a woman has a child and no man around the home, another man may take an interest in her child but the woman sometimes take that as a sign of daddy, father, or husband. That's when their emotions override them and they become emotionally attached. So now, before a man godfather's or mentors a child, he has to sit down with the single mother first and let her know that this is no wise a door for him to come into her home or life, but to give an investment to the child.

Can't Handle the Truth

Tony F.: Women are so easily frustrated when men don't express themselves verbally. It's a war, at times, because a lot of women want to hear us say things but when we say them, they may not be reflective of their truth. They want to hear certain things come from you but they don't really want to hear what you have to say. If you aren't saying what they want to hear, they become easily frustrated.

Larry: They say, "Don't lie to me." But when you tell the truth they want to crucify you.

Clifford: When you tell them the truth, 90% of the time they don't believe you.

Eric: They want to close their eyes to the truth. They'd rather be ignorant to things. It's almost like they want you to lie to them.

Mark: Sometimes men aren't truthful because they don't feel as though they can be. Men can be very truthful, almost to the point of being raw, but they have to constantly make sure that is channeled in a way that will not cause a woman to go into some dramatic emotional act.

Deceptive

Gerald: A lot of women send out mixed signals. One minute they are staring into your eyes like you two are the only two on earth. Yet, when you approach them to pursue the attraction, they inform you that they aren't interested or that they are married.

Lydell: Women keep a lot of secrets. They don't always open up, or they aren't truthful about their feelings on certain issues. That brings about dishonesty and deception.

Arnold: Some women can be very cunning. They have a way of manipulating people and situations without their deceit being obvious.

Chau: Some women know how to put on airs and pretend to be something they're not. I don't like fake women with fake smiles.

Richard C.: Some women lie and pretend to be something that they aren't just to impress me. Be up front about who you really are. If you lie to me, I'll never have a reason to trust you.

Greg: Women hide their true selves to get a man. Once they get married or into a committed relationship, things change slightly or in a major way. Because women have a need to be in a committed relationship, they hide who they truly are at first.

Ryan: To me, in relationships, you have to be honest with who you are upfront. Then, you won't have a fear of being found out. I think women sometimes aren't really being who they are, especially in the early stages of the relationship. After you are together for a while, she starts to break down. She can't keep up certain facades anymore. You then realize there is something about her that you might not be so crazy about. Whereas, if she was upfront at the beginning, you might find that you need somebody who actually suites you better. Women should be themselves and not who they think you want them to be, or who they want you to think they are.

Manipulative

Michael W.: Some women are not honest. They can be manipulative and come with a preconceived agenda.

Julian: Some women aren't really interested in you for yourself. They have ulterior motives.

Robert C.: Some women want you to get in the middle of family disputes. She'll ask you for your opinion but the problem comes when you do give your opinion and you don't give the one that she wants to hear. You have to tell her what she wants to hear or she will cause a problem. She shouldn't expect me to always be on her side just because I want to be with her. That's manipulation.

Gerry: It's really negative when I tell you key things about myself-- my likes, dislikes, my wants, needs, weaknesses, the things that will hurt me, and you use them as a form of manipulation against me to benefit yourself.

Ty: I call it "Operation Pressure." You meet someone, hang out for a while, and everything is going A-Okay. All of a sudden- out of the blue, you find yourself having to make a commitment. You're like—"Where did this come from?" They more or less want a commitment. They want to settle down and once they established that is what they want to do, there's only two things left for her to do-- get pregnant or married, one of the two. It doesn't matter which comes first. They aren't picky about what comes first but one of them has to happen. A lot of women are in pursuit of settling down, getting married, and having children. Nothing is wrong with that except they become overly consumed with it and expect it to happen in a short period of time with someone they hardly know. They want a commitment too soon and start playing games to get one. There are some women who don't necessarily want a commitment, they just want some kind of tie to you so that anytime they call you, you'll come. That's manipulation.

Too Involved With Others

Mamy: Women can sometimes be too open to the conditions of others. They get too involved in others' lives and take on their burdens. They become consumed and overwhelmed with their problems. This creates a negative impact on their personal relationship.

Ronald: A lot of women get too involved in what is going on in the lives of their girlfriends. They want to bring her problems into the home or relationship.

Nayoti: That's true. That time your mate needs is lacking because you're giving too much time to someone else.

Julian: Some women are more involved with their friends, family, or they are more involved with their children. They have less time to spend with their man. A man may feel that she has no time for him. Time becomes an issue because not enough quality time is spent together.

Patrick: For a lot of women, children are their only focus. Most mothers seem to be more attentive of the kids, and not so much towards the husband after the kids are born. A lot of times, the husband goes by the wayside and his needs are no longer met. At that stage, communication between the man and the woman gets halted. She makes the kids her only or main priority and focus.

Jesse: Women's minds are sometimes in other places. They are easily persuaded by church people, friends, girlfriends, family members, and other things they are involved in. They make things outside of the relationship a higher priority. It's like- "I'll do what I have to do and when I'm finished, I will call him." It's as if the man should just sit by and wait until she is finished solving life's problems.

Switches Up

Melvin: If a woman pays attention to her man, she will see what he likes, wants, and needs. A lot of women see your wants, likes, and needs, and start off fulfilling them. Then, all of a sudden, they change and begin to take you for granted. They're like, "I don't' want to do that anymore." Your response is- "What do you mean you don't want to do that? Doing that was part of my attraction to you." A woman may know how to get a man but a lot of women don't know how to keep a man. They pull you in under false pretenses. Once they have you wide open- they change it all up!

Jesse: Some women perpetrate a fraud. You talk to them about things that you desire out of the relationship and they say that they understand what it is you are looking for. After you get involved with them, you soon find out that they really don't understand. When you first meet them, you can have long discussions about situations and how you want them, but farther down the road, at times, they act like you are just meeting them for the first time. Most women start out with giving 100%. They go down to 70%, then 20%, then they give only 10%. At first, they are right there for you. Once they have you-- it's like you become their yo-yo. For instance, when we first met and began a relationship everything was fine. We're supposed to meet at 3:30, at 3:30 you're there. A couple of months later you get there at 3:40. A week after that you get there at 3:50. You got me now. As long as you have me where you want me, you get there when you feel good and ready. I'm not as important in the middle of the relationship as I was in the beginning. They switch up and the real them comes out.

Uses Sex as a Weapon

Roosevelt: Some women hold back physically and emotionally on their husbands for whatever reasons they feel are justified.

Kenneth: Women often use sex as a weapon, a tool, or a commodity. When she feels that the man hasn't done what she expects him to do, then she'll hold back. All bets are off.

Mark: Women use sex as a weapon and they use it as a controlling factor. For instance- "Honey, clean the driveway and then we can do this tonight." Well, no. I'm not a horse and you're not dangling carrots (sex) in front of me. They underestimate the intellect of a man in that regard. They think we're supposed to be these hyper sexual individuals who only have this one thing on our minds. They fail to realize this is a rather demeaning way to treat men. Men are not as dumb or nearly as desperate as women believe them to be.

Patrick: Some women use sex as a weapon and hold it over their husband's head. If you don't comply with their wishes, they will withhold sex. That's a big turn-off. I don't think sex should ever be brought up as a tool- a manipulating tool. I think both people really need that. It's a bond between the two. It bonds and completes that intimacy package. Without it, it won't work. I think the marriage will eventually fall apart and they will go their separate ways. Too many women use sex as a manipulation tool- as a weapon.

Indirectness

Jermaine H. In general, I think men are simpler in how they look at things. Women are a little more complex. Men look at things systematically and try to come up with solutions, whereas some women just want to talk and not come to a particular conclusion or solution. So, trying to understand what it is that they really want can sometimes become a very complex situation.

Larry: I have a major problem with how indirect women can be. You have to decode what they're trying to say to you.

Gary: Yeah, you have to read between the lines and try to figure out what they are *really* trying to say.

Clifford: Yeah! They don't want you to play mind games but they're always playing mind games with you.

Larry: There is a lot of decoding you have to do if you are a guy. Women can't see that at all. Whenever she is upset, you have to figure out if it's me, her parents, or the job. But she comes at me, even though it might not be about me. Somehow, in my questioning it, it becomes about me.

Gary: Then you have to be the mind reader all over again.

Larry: Right, right! They say you should know this,

you should know that. Well-- how about you telling me *this*? How about you tell me in words what's bothering you? When some women are mad, you usually get the stare-"You know what I'm talking about." And when you ask what's wrong it's-"Nothing". Okay, what is it?

Gary: Tell us what you want. We are not mind readers. Let us know, help us out. Talk to us. Don't make me try to guess what's on your mind.

Larry: That's where the indirectness comes about. They're not really being themselves. They're not thinking the way they should think. They are thinking, "How do you think I should think?" But we can't' figure out what they think we think they should be thinking. It shouldn't be any strategy involved. Just say what's on your mind.

Lennie: A lot of times, men have to have some kind of decoding mechanism when a woman talks-"What are you saying? I don't understand that. Let me decode this message." That's what it seems like we have to do. This is a great issue in the male community. We have secret meetings about how women ask questions that make men look at women like-"This does not compute. I understand not. Where are you coming from? Why would you ask me that? Let me decode that- de, de, de, boop, boop, boop—oh now I understand!" They look at that as rejection. It's not rejection on our part. We just don't know how to answer you. A lot of what they have to say needs decoding and we don't always know how to decode messages when they are indirect.

Ryan: Women may try, in their own way, to let you know how they feel about things, even though they may not always be clear. I think men are more straightforward and direct about things. Women have more of an ambiguous nature of expressing something, at times. Men are much more likely, in my experience, to say-"I don't like this, I don't want this. This is making me happy." Men usually tell you what's going on- once you get them talking. Women tend to want the man to figure out on his own by dropping hints-things like that. That is frustrating. A lot of women sort of feel that you should know how they feel or you should know what they want. I feel that you should never assume how someone feels or what they want. I am a believer in open communication and coming straight out and saying something as opposed to dropping hints, alluding to something, and expecting you to try to figure it out. You can't bet on anyone to be able to read your mind. That leaves it open for a lot of misinterpretation and miscommunication which I believe is one of the biggest problems in relationships. Don't make assumptions. Be clear about your goals, what you want and how you feel. Just say in black and white terms- "This is how I feel, this is what I want." They are counting on men to make those assumptions for them and they are setting themselves up for failure. Women should be more straight forward and honest about what they really want.

Verbally Offensive

Scott: When some women get angry, they sometimes use the man's physical parts to berate or belittle him.

Roosevelt: Nagging. I don't care for a woman who nags.

Malcolm: Some women are always using profanity. People get upset and say a few bad words, but if you're cursing every time you breathe, that's a turn-off to me.

Robert C.: It's negative when the woman communicates with me like I'm a thug on the street or one of her girlfriends.

Jesse: Very negative is a bossy and mouthy woman who butts in my conversations when I'm talking to someone else. A loud, big-mouthed woman is a turn-off. You'll talk to them about certain things and they'll be wrong, but they still run their mouths It just leads to an argument. Instead of saying, "Yeah, you're right."- they run their mouths about something that is irrelevant or not true.

Malcolm: Some women can be loud and wrong. They may not have all the facts together but you can't tell them they're wrong. They insist on being right all the time.

Daryl: Some women have a way of saying things to their husbands that come off as though they are speaking down to them. It's almost like they are talking to a child. I don't think they realize how or what they are saying. The little criticisms can be very hard to take from the wife.

Clifford: When the woman talks to me like I'm a child, my mind is saying, "Why is she talking to me like I'm a child?"

Gary: Yeah! When they talk to us like a child, it makes us feel as if we're stupid. They can talk to us like we're stupid.

Julian: There is a double standard as far as listening. They want us to listen to them but we can say nothing. I don't know what that is about. Some women have bad attitudes which reflect in constant yelling and snapping.

Rick W.: I can't take the hollering, screaming type of women. These women get bent out of shape over dumb stuff. Any woman who feels that she has to scream, yell, and rant, has no idea of the negativity she is projecting.

Ty: A woman with an argumentative spirit is very offensive and negative to me. A lot of women will try to push your buttons and get you all hyped up just to see how far you will go. They'll try to argue by saying a little something and adding a little stuff. It's like they just want you to blow up. It's like they are just waiting to get an argument started.

Jermaine T.: Some women don't know how to communicate so they'll start arguing with you. They think they communicate better when they argue. They don't know how to communicate on a positive level, to voice their opinions to get an understanding, or to discuss what's really going on. They'd rather argue with you and cause a little ruckus.

Trevor: You're right! But the arguments, most of the time, aren't about what you're arguing about. It's about something else that they don't really want to bring up or talk about. It's about something they've contrived in their minds and ran with, but with all the arguing you still don't resolve anything.

Jermaine T.: Yeah, if a situation occurs that needs to be dealt with, deal with it and leave it alone. We've already discussed the issue but she wants to bring it up again in the next conversation.

Trevor: That's true, and if we're trying to communicate, especially if it's about something that she did wrong, she shouldn't get mad at me for getting mad about what she did wrong.

Lennie: Some women need to restrain what comes out of their mouths. They need to be mindful of what and how they say things. A lot of conflict and confusion occur when the woman feels as though she needs to go tit for tat with the man. He says one thing and she just has to respond. She has to have the last word. Women have a tendency to say the same thing over and over. They need to learn how to say what they feel or what they need to say just once, and then leave it alone. Let it go. It would create a more pleasant environment and encourage better communication.

James: Women don't know when to shut up. They think they have this inalienable right to say whatever it is they want to say, when they want to say it, for however long they want to say it, and you're supposed to just stand there and listen to them.

Too Picky

Chau: 9 times out of 10, a woman will choose a so called "good-looking" guy over a so-called "average looking" one. They don't realize that a lot of very attractive men are players or dogs. The right guy can be right in front of them but they don't want him. They are too caught up in looks and then wonder why their relationship is superficial, causing many problems to occur within the relationship.

Trevor: In my mind, one of the problems with relationships is that women complain that they can't find a good man, "All men are dogs." All these women know good men, yet 9 times out of 10, they'll choose the messed-up man and try to convert him into a good man. There's a good man standing right there, though.

Jermaine T.: Yeah, but they want Pookie. Pookie is an old drunk but they're going to fix him up. A good man is right there but I guess he's too easy. They want more of a challenge. Is that what it is?

Trevor: That's part of it, but then they'll complain how the guy mistreats them because they didn't take into consideration the type of man they went after, the type of man they've allowed into their circle. They seem to keep going after the same type of man. They don't want to try someone different. They are too picky.

Kleinberg: I find that there are 30 and 40 year-old women walking around asking, "Why can't I find a man?" The problem I have is that there are men everywhere but no one is good enough for them. They find character flaws with everybody. If they can find a car, a dress, a job, or a house to their specifications, why can't they find a mate? The reason why there are so many single women is because a lot of them sit back and pick and pick and pick. They want everything to perfection. They aren't willing to work at relationships anymore because they want instant perfection. A lot of women are single because they are too critical, too fault-finding, and expect perfection in their mate, even though they are imperfect. They are just too picky.

Easily Persuaded By Girlfriends

Duane: Women, a lot of times, are sharing with their girlfriends and everyone except their man. Maybe they feel that men wouldn't understand what they are going through. They feel women understand more because of their commonalities so they share more with other females. That can be a misapprehension. Men understand a lot more than they are given credit for and should be given more opportunities to give their input and insight on issues that pertain to them both.

Sylvester: Some women need to give more attention to their relationship. Too often, they rely on the experience of their girlfriends and allow them to supposedly give them helpful hints or advice about the relationship. She tries to use her stuff on you and it doesn't always work. Her experience or suggestions may not fit your situation. It's almost like they say to your woman, "Girl, do this. I did this to my man and now I have him in check, under control, so you need to try this." In a lot of cases, that advice has backfired because she didn't pay enough attention to her man to know that some things won't work on him, even if it worked for her girlfriend's relationship.

Robert C: What goes on between you and me should stay between us. If it's not life threatening, don't go to your girlfriends. That's the most negative thing a woman can do. You don't need to run to your girlfriends and tell them everything we do. They allow the girlfriend to have too much influence on them, especially if the girlfriend does not have a companion and you two are getting along.

Michael W.: It's really negative when the girlfriend relationship is closer than the marital relationship as far as confidentiality. Many women feel they should be able to share anything they want regarding their husbands, or their actions with their husbands, even without his knowledge. Some feel that it's none of his business, anyway. I think it is inappropriate, unethical, and a lot of ugly things happen when women take private issues outside of the house, or anything they know their spouse prefers to be kept confidential, and share it with their girlfriends.

"The wise woman builds her house; the foolish one pulls it down with her own hands."
Proverbs 14:1

Three: Her Influence on the Relationship

The scripture quoted above emphasizes the great impact and influence women have on relationships. Such knowledge should inspire women to utilize their skills and graces to enhance the relationship and help to keep it on an **even keel.**.

I wonder if those skills and graces are sometimes compromised, causing her to linger too long in a lopsided relationship. I wonder if the relationship is lopsided because she's not fully convinced of the power she has to rise up and make the demands on the relationship that will keep it **equally gratifying and mutually satisfying**. Because of the supposed "male shortage," I wonder if the reasoning of- *"At least I have a man!"* is enough for her. I also wonder how that particular reasoning has caused her to settle in areas and relationships far beneath her worth.

Women, we must never underestimate the great value and high worth attributed to the female nature. With it comes tremendous power and influence that can be used as a barometer to detect the counterfeits who may ultimately exploit us by minimizing our influence and rendering our impact subservient to theirs.

Please know, according to the scripture quoted above, we are deemed an influential and impactful people. You must also know that it is in our hands to utilize our power, influence, and impact for the good or bad, for the building up or tearing down.

What impact or influence do women have on relationships?

Maurice: Women are the driving force in most relationships. They actually guide the relationships, a lot of times- in a lot of ways. For instance, I don't like to celebrate holidays but my wife will not allow that. If I'm not on board with that, it's going to be chaos in the house. So, just to keep the peace, I have to get on board. That is just one example of how women drive or guide relationships.

Kevin: The woman has a major impact on the relationship. A woman's emotions can break or make the relationship. Back to that word emotional- a woman's emotions can tear up anything by the way she sees and perceives it to be. Whether it's right or wrong, her reactions to it can either solve the problem or cause the problem.

Gerry: They are the impact. A woman can disturb the house or bring calm to the house.

Michael W.: The energy that they put into sustaining the relationship is amazing! Also, the thoughtfulness and forethought that go into making the relationship optimal is truly amazing. The energy of the emotional investment women put into the relationship impacts it for the greater! It's fascinating!

Bill: Women, I feel, always hold all the cards and call all the shots. Men want to make women happy. From that perspective, their self-worth or their happiness is based on the happiness of the woman they are with, and the women in their lives. I think an unhappy woman in a relationship makes for an unhappy relationship. That is the huge influence the woman has on the relationship.

Aaron: Women set the tone of the relationship and the home. Men generally respond to the atmosphere or environment that she has created.

Christopher: Women have a significant impact. So much to the point that based on their background and where they're from, they can literally define the relationship.

Gregory: Women are major influences on relationships. Where they are coming from in terms of past experiences, where they are currently, and what direction they desire the relationship to go in, all impact the success of the relationship. Oftentimes, women are more devoted to the relationship, therefore, they bring strong commitment to the relationship.

Scott: Women have a lot of power. A woman can make you feel like you're on top of the world, and then she can turn around and make you feel like you are on the bottom of a shoe. She can say something to you that will make you feel like there's nothing in the world better than that moment and that time of being with her. At other times, she can make you feel so low. They have a strong impact on how you feel about yourself.

Timothy: A woman who is together in the assertiveness of her worth and esteem has a major influence on the success of the relationship.

Joe: I think women will look for deeper relationships sooner than men will, therefore, they pretty much steer the course many times. They definitely have a greater impact in the initial stages because they pretty much decide if the relationship will go to the next level.

Tony D.: Women have a great impact on the relationship because they are very persuasive in the decision- making process.

James: Women are major influences on the relationship. It works well when women know their place, their strengths, and their position. When a woman understands what Godly Order is, knows the necessity of being lined up properly, and understands the role women played in Scripture; how God has given women a very unique role, a very diverse role, and a very important role in making or breaking the relationship, she is well on her way to making the relationship optimal. I think the stronger the woman, the stronger the relationship. They definitely are major influences on the relationship.

Leroy: Women can foster a certain disposition in the relationship that can create an antagonistic relationship, or they can create a "work-together" relationship; whereas each partner combines their thoughts and ideas before reaching a conclusion. Also, her interactions can influence or encourage a certain change in what he says, does, or how he interacts.

Richard W.: Women bring positive direction to the relationship. Most men are not stable. A good woman stabilizes him and neutralizes that aggressiveness that makes him want to travel to see other things, possibly other women. She encourages him to focus on all that they have accomplished together, and what they have with each other as partners in life. Also, the woman can add to the relationship if she has a man who is introverted but she is extroverted. She can bring out the qualities he has hidden inside because of his shyness. Her positive influence could help to draw him out of himself.

Michael L.: Women are the glue that keeps the relationship together. Women have so much more unseen authority over men than men have over women. Most men can lift heavier, run faster, and can do physical feats much stronger, but at the end of the day, at the end of an issue, women have much more authority over men. They can control men by their emotions more than they realize they can. They can keep us in check and let us know when we went too far to the left or too far to the right. They can put us in our place. I don't think men really realize that until later on in life. This whole journey through life we are thinking that we are on top and that we are the victors, but women have been really controlling us the whole time.

Kleinberg: They bring a strong emotional component to the relationship that a lot of men are lacking and that is required. They bring a lot of intimacy, a lot of support. Women pick up the pieces or fill in the missing links where they are needed in your life. They make the relationship.

Richard C: The woman impacts the relationship by being there emotionally, physically, spiritually, and mentally. The relationship is not complete if she leaves out any of those components. She is the most important person in the relationship because she adds all those qualities: emotional, mental, spiritual, and physical stability. Her positive influence will inspire him to take the initiative to do what he needs to do.

Carroll: Women bring special emotional qualities to the relationship. They display their emotions more than men do. Whether it's verbal, whether it is a touch, whether it is actions, they hold it together through the emotional. They bring a whole level of emotions that men just aren't in touch with as much.

David: Women drive the relationship. A man just

needs to feel comfortable and welcomed. If he does, he will do what a woman wants or needs to be done. He will do what it takes to keep her happy when she makes him feel secure, welcomed, accepted, and appreciated. Women have a huge impact in driving the relationship, and getting the results they desire from their man.

"You are all fair my love, and there is no spot in you."
Song of Solomon 4:7

Four: My Ideal Woman

Most women create in their minds the image of their so-called "perfect man". For a lot of these women, when they enter into a new relationship and the man doesn't reflect the pre-conceived image of their "perfect man", very often, they will set off on a course of action to help him conform to the image of their "perfect man".

Well, maybe- just maybe- her man has an image of the so-called "ideal woman," and maybe-- I'm only suggesting that maybe- she doesn't measure up to his image.

I don't know how fair it is that we get to express to the world, our parents, best friends, colleagues, co-workers, and anyone else who will listen, who and what we want our "perfect man" to be, and not hold ourselves accountable to become what he may want or desire us to be.

Let me be clear, I do not believe that a person should give up his individuality to appease the relationship, but I do believe that both persons should make the personal adjustments needed so that true gratification is **evenly dispersed** throughout the relationship. For, every relationship should come with a set of established ideals to strive towards. Having such ideals will ensure that each person will be inspired to maximize their potential to achieve the optimal within the relationship.

Therefore, to achieve balance and equality, it is only fair that our men are afforded the same opportunity to create and express their image of the "ideal woman". I don't mean ideal in the sense of a "perfect woman", but ideal in the sense of being the "most suitable partner" for him.

Let's level the playing field by putting their ideals on the table. Not to make any woman feel insecure about who she is, but to inspire each other to fulfill the **desire of the other**, thus becoming to **one another-** the **"perfect man"** and the **"ideal woman."**

Create the image of your ideal woman:

Kevin: My ideal woman is a woman who knows who she is, and has learned to live single. There's a different kind of relationship when you have a female who is all about a man versus a female who is very confident and knows herself. She's a woman who has goals and ambitions. She has a relationship with God. She knows what she wants. She knows where she wants to go and does not mind going for it, and she allows her man to help her get there. An ideal woman is a strong, confident woman.

Gerald: My ideal woman is one who knows how to put me in my place when I need to be reminded of it. She will not back down from me when I'm wrong. She would uplift me when I need it. She would grow with me spiritually.

Christopher: My ideal woman would first and foremost believe in Jesus Christ, and be led by the Holy Spirit. With that, the Lord will have other things in place, such as her role as the woman and allowing me to fulfill my role as the man. She would allow me to make some decisions, even though from her perspective they might be the wrong choices. She would still allow me that space to make them. If I fail, she would encourage me to grow and learn from the mistakes. An ideal woman would allow me some sort of individuality. She would allow me to enjoy some things on my own, without her. She knows how to be in my company without smothering me or wanting me to be up under her.

Joseph: A praying woman who loves God as much as I love Him. She would be very in tune with me spiritually. She would know how to hold me when I need to be held. She would listen to me and seek to understand me.

Michael W.: A Bible Believer. She is a person who does not allow cultural issues to affect her faith. Christianity is Christianity. It has nothing to do with where you live, what time it is, or what period of history it is. Its rules, edicts, and expectations don't change. An ideal woman is open, honest, and a true confidant.

Tony D.: One who is spiritual-minded, and is willing to work by your side to accomplish great feats in life. She's a spiritually aggressive woman who knows how to use the Word of God to put me in check, to bring calm to my life. She is a very sensual woman. She is confident in herself and what she can do.

Will: I seek out personality and intelligence before physical beauty. She is someone who I can develop a friendship with, someone who I can easily communicate with.

Rodney: My ideal woman is spiritual. She is observant, nurturing, stern, yet flexible. She has an awareness of who she is, who she really is. Because she is aware of who she is, she's made plans for where she wants to go in life. She is educated. I don't mean she has to be a college graduate. She may not be educated scholastically, but educated in terms of knowing how to properly handle whatever situation she encounters. She has equipped herself with the knowledge and skills necessary to survive any ordeal.

Duane: One who is caring, sharing, and nurturing. Sharing is so important in a relationship in terms of establishing good communication. An ideal woman is God-fearing. She's a woman who has great self-esteem and self-worth. She is a woman who wants to be cherished, and who respects her significant other. She is willing to do anything for him, as long as it is not illegal, unethical, immoral, or doesn't break the laws of God or man.

Ty: I like one who can cook, and I mean a home-cooked meal. Eating out is fine, but I personally prefer home- cooked meals. You can't put a price tag on a good home-cooked meal.

Julian: My ideal woman would understand her man. Men will always want to be physical with the woman they love, in any way possible; a hug, affection, a kiss. My ideal woman would know that. She understands what a man wants, the ideas of a man, the reasoning of a man, and why men do certain things.

Leroy: A woman who is comfortable with her man being a man. A woman with whom a man can say how he feels and what he thinks without having to tailor it so that it won't give the wrong emotional impact. The ideal woman would be able to decipher what a man is saying or feeling. She is concerned with pleasing her husband. She would understand men's viewpoints, how they come across, and how they carry themselves. She would consult with her man but allow him to make the final decisions.

Kleinberg: Little things make her happy. She's not easily bothered but easy-going. Some women are so high-strung that everything bothers them. Anything can set them off. My ideal woman is someone who loves life, people, especially children. She is always happy and positive.

Gilbert: My wife. My ideal woman has ambitions, desires, motivations, and intellect.

Eric: A woman who has her own mind.

Richard C.: My ideal woman would have my back. When I discuss a plan with her, she will back me up. She is a woman who is giving. She loves people. She's not too flashy or too pompous. She is affectionate. She is very affectionate and doesn't mind hugging you in the middle of the mall or in the supermarket. She'll even pull over on the highway just to give me a hug.

Reuben: Someone with whom you can grow, someone who augments you, and you can depend on her.

Chau: My ideal woman is very caring. Caring is very important to me. How she cares for me tells me how much she really loves me.

Sylvester: She is all into me. She is so mad about me that she makes me feel safe and secure. She makes me feel that I am the one! That makes a difference in the relationship. Even though she may find someone that others feel is better than me, she always lets me know that I am the one. Also, my ideal woman is beautiful in many ways. She mainly possesses an inner beauty that allows her to communicate with me on many levels. She is a well-rounded person. She's someone I can flow with, talk with, and experience new adventures with.

Malcolm: My ideal woman is fun-loving, adventurous, and spontaneous. She will be ready to go at a moment's notice.

Larry: A woman who has a sense of humor. She's well-read. She doesn't have to have the same opinions as me but she has to be able to substantiate hers. Smart women are a huge turn-on.

Arnold: An ideal woman is a good conversationalist. She is conversant with life issues and current events.

Robert C.: Talking. I like talking. She is someone I can talk to about everything- from sports to politics. That excites me. I get a lot from conversation. It's like a turn-on.

Gary: My wife. Even though she is an independent woman, we enjoy being together and sharing different experiences. We are able to discuss any topic or issue.

Michael R.: My ideal woman has a strong and positive inner self. She has the ability to always look on the brighter side of things. She can discern the good things of life, and create ways to make those good things appear so that our life together is pleasant and peaceful. I'm not suggesting that unpleasant situations won't occur, or that you'll never have to deal with serious issues, but you're better able to cope with them when you're mentally prepared. Situations won't be so stressful when you are mentally prepared for them. The ideal woman prepares herself mentally by maintaining a positive attitude about life.

Aaron: A loving and genuine person, one who I can envision as the mother of my child, my best friend, my lover. I can envision her as my wife, but most of all, my best friend. My ideal woman would relate to me. She would listen to me with her heart and soul. She's a person who understands and accepts my manhood. She will respect it and not insult it. For instance, she would not say to me "If you were a man, you would..." It's not like I had a father or grandfather who molded me, or helped to shape me into the man I need to be. I'm taking bits and pieces from men who I think are great and trying to mold myself to be a great man in her life. She would understand that and wouldn't ever insult my manhood.

Gerry: A woman who looked in the mirror that morning and felt good about herself. She walks with a sense of confidence. She's articulate, intelligent, and inspiring. If she is not happy in a particular area, she makes goals to do better and she's achieving her goals. Definitely, she is artistic. I love jazz and plays. I love to get out of the house. I love spontaneity. She's aggressive. She has her own mind, own place, own abilities, and a strong sense of family structure. She is absolutely loving and super affectionate. She is exciting and excitable. You can talk to her about any subject under the sun without her getting offended. She would receive me in all areas.

Tony F.: Strength, her internal strength. Her motor-what's driving her? What's keeping her going? What's keeping her fire lit for life? Her intestinal fortitude- I love a female who can carry on! An ideal woman has her own thing that she does. She can be an athlete, a teacher, whatever. For me, the ideal woman is one who is into poetry and spirituality. She's earthy, spiritual, honest, and receptive. She would be humorous, adventurous, active, rich-- not with money but with experiences. She's had an opportunity to try the waters in different places and now she's figuring out that she needs someone as real as her. That's ideal! She's one who loves life for what it is. She's someone who is not there for money, not there for glamour. She's just there to live life!

Travis: My ideal woman is positive and ambitious. She desires things out of life and is willing to work hard to obtain them. She is very secure with herself; her physical appearance, her station in life. She doesn't complain a lot. She makes things happen for her and others. She likes to be treated well. She likes to treat her man well. She is real. She has a desire to grow with her man. It endears me when I feel that my woman is really into me. I don't feel stressed around her, therefore, I can let my hair down, so to speak. It makes me say "That lady is cool. She's okay. I love being around her!"

Rick W.: My ideal woman is like a one-stop shop! Everything you need or want can be found in her. She would be my buddy, my lover, my friend, my girl, my partner, my "every woman." She'll desire to become my fantasy, within reason of course, without compromising her integrity. I won't need to venture out, to go anywhere else, or to anyone else to get any of my needs met! She'll be my one-stop shop!

"Let us lay aside every weight and the sin which so easily ensnares us."
Hebrews 12:1

Five: Her Emotional Baggage

The basis for this next question needs very little explanation or commentary. The question itself attests to the importance of its responses.

However, when two people enter into a relationship, both persons come with their own history, own past, or series of events that have culminated into the person they are presently. Attempting to blend the histories together can sometimes be complicated or difficult; because each history, each past, every series of events bring with them a psychological and emotional component. The episodes which have adversely affected the emotional or psychological capacities, if not sufficiently dealt with or adequately resolved, will inadvertently, in a negative way, determine the outcome or dictate the climate of the new relationship you are trying to establish.

You see, we can only use the tools we garnered

through our experiences and observations. If those tools have been acquired through faulty learning and bad experiences, we are rendered ill-equipped to withstand the pressures and challenges the new relationship may present us with.

Therefore, we must do the work to make the changes due that will settle and resolve the issues of the past and present. However, before we can do the work, we must ***first recognize, acknowledge, and accept*** that there ***are*** issues adversely impacting our emotional and psychological capacities. Any lack of recognition, acknowledgement, or acceptance of such, will only hinder us from intimately bonding with the current man in our lives.

What are some psychological or emotional factors that hinder the woman from intimately bonding with her man? In other words, what baggage do women bring to the relationship?

Menstruation

Mamy: One emotional factor is menstruation. Women go through a lot of changes and moods during their menstrual cycle. If they don't have their emotions in check, they can make it very unbearable for the man. They need to deal with their emotional state during menstruation and not use it as an excuse for being cranky and irritable. Their mood swings cause the man to go through too many unnecessary changes.

Fear of Dependency

Daryl: Women have a fear of being vulnerable to men and developing a dependency on them. As a result, they really don't know how to bond with a man. I think there are two reasons for that- some men don't know how to be an authority in the home, and the other reason is that women had to become independent because of bad relationships and single- parent families. They didn't have a role model in the home and it causes them to fear being dependent on a man.

Christopher: A lot of women do not allow men to be the head of the household. In a lot of cases, women have not been shown or taught what the role of a man is. They have no idea of his role. She has no clue. How could she? There was no man present in her home to model the role of a man. Therefore, most men experience a woman who will take care of everything. That's been the role of her mother and that's the role that she assumes. If she is not careful, her fear of dependency will cause her to take control and run the relationship as the man and the woman.

Chau: Being equal to a man is not enough for some women. It seems that a lot of women today cross the line by trying to take the place of a man because they fear being dependent on him.

Darin: Some women need to be careful of an independent spirit. There's nothing wrong with being self-sufficient. I think both partners have to bring something to the relationship. They both have to be able to handle finances and handle situations individually, but a lot of women today want to be independent all the way around. They don't want to depend on a man for anything. A man's purpose in life is to take care of the woman, to be the head of the household, to take care of his family. Nowadays, women want to take over that role and shun men away. They try to be too dominant in the relationship but it is not supposed to be that way. I think they fear being too dependent on a man.

Emotionally Depleted

Christopher: The whole concept of "I need a man" and not "I want a man"-meaning that you would do anything to get a man. When they get the wrong type of man, and finally get to the point where they decide that they've had enough of his abuse, whether it was physical or emotional abuse, the damage has already been done. They've spent several years with him, borne two or three children with him, and now they are emotionally spent and physically drained. When they get into the next relationship, they don't have much to offer or to give.

Mark: Women, a lot of times, put on a type of front to deflect things that could possibly hurt them, like intimate feelings. They reason-"I've been hurt before so I don't need this, I don't need that. I don't need a man for anything." They become so emotionally depleted that they become numb to their feelings. That's a sad way to be in life.

Jermaine T.: Women shouldn't work so hard on the job until they're too tired to take care of home or family. Don't give all of yourself to your job. Save some for your family.

Chau: I think that many women today are trying to compete with men and it is causing a breakdown in the family. I'm not saying that a woman's place is only in the home, but a lot of women are overworked and it causes problems in the home. If they made better choices about their mates, they would not have to overwork themselves.

Duncan: I think work could be baggage. Some women are so focused on their careers that the relationship may not go anywhere until they have their career set where they want it. That focus causes them to be overworked, overly stressed, and often emotionally unavailable. Therefore, they can't give the relationship the time and effort it needs to bond.

Mark: Society has marketed women to become all things to all people. Women have been bombarded with a litany of materials that suggest they can be all things. How does it go? - "I can bring home the bacon and fry it in the pan." These unrealistic expectations they put on themselves, as well as society in general, have made them overworked and overtired, leaving them emotionally depleted.

Will: Some women are obsessed with work. They may have taken a job before you two met and they put more focus on that job than trying to get to know the person they are getting into a relationship with. The job consumes most of their time. It makes it difficult to get to know the new person she is trying to get with.

Julian: A lot of women think that they are the only ones who have emotional or psychological problems. Men, sometimes, have those problems, too. Every woman has problems, they're there. The real problem is her creating more problems in the relationship because of her problems. For instance, "Work didn't go well today, I'm in a bad mood." She comes home snapping and yelling. "I don't feel like doing this, I don't feel like doing that." Men are like, "Are you going to be in a bad mood the rest of your life?" Most of the time, men like to be happy or stress free. They will do things to maintain happiness and alleviate stress. If you're constantly coming home with all the problems and unhappiness of the day, and go on and on and on about all the problems at work, he'll become frustrated, depressed, and will feel like he has to leave the house for a while just to get some peace. Because she is emotionally depleted from the stress at work, she makes it hard to maintain peace in the home.

Single Parenthood

Duncan: Unfortunately, being a single parent can be baggage brought to a relationship. For single mothers, they not only have to consider themselves in a relationship but they have to consider their children, also. They have to consider what affect children may have on the relationship and the impact the relationship might have on the children. They have to consider if the man will even accept her children or be willing to deal with her children. These are baggage that can weigh the relationship down.

Sexual Abuse

Ty: Many women have been sexually abused by someone in their family; an uncle, father, stepfather, or brother. If they are not strong minded to the point where they can fight off the fears and hurts of what they went through, they often become promiscuous. Because they didn't get help when they needed it, they end up demeaning themselves by sleeping with many men. Then no *one* man can satisfy them.

Hooper: Some women carry the baggage of having been raped. Some carry the baggage of being molested by a family member. Some carry the baggage of hearing- "You're no good and you will never be anything." Therefore, it is hard for that woman to conceive that she is worthy of the love a good man, especially if she was sexually abused. That makes it hard for her to bond with a man.

Physical Abuse

Alex: It could be past issues with other people or other events. I was told about a woman whose boyfriend was extremely physically abusive. So much so, that now, even though she has moved away and is with someone else, she can't actually have a child. She keeps miscarrying. Her past physical abuse affects her current relationship.

Personality Disorders

Aaron: Personality, attitudes-- tone them down. Every situation doesn't have to be chaotic, to the extreme, or excessive. Let some things roll off your back. Women don't know how to get over things quickly.

Rodney: The way women articulate or speak should not depend on the setting. A woman shouldn't be like Dr. Jekyll and Mr. Hyde. They have to realize that how they are at home should be the same way they are in the streets. They should always be respectful. She should be who she is 25 hours a day, 8 days a week. There is no "work face" or "home face." You spend the majority of time in the home. Your behavior, your practice, and your nature become habitual. Why should you put on a facade when you go to work?

Ty: Too many women have personalities where we have to test what personality they are wearing that day. You have the emotional type of personality where nothing is going right. You're depressed, and go on and on about how nothing is going right. And you have the- "I am a real witch today." Mad for no reason, yet there is a reason, we just don't know the reason. She is mad and frustrated but won't let us know why. We're left baffled- "Dang, why is she so mad? What did I do?" Next, you have the- "I gotta have it." The nympho type. That's all she wants- but just for that day. She's all up under you and all over you. So, basically, you have to test to see which personality she is wearing that day. The first two moods make you just want to split and not be around them. I don't like to argue so I just learned to say up front- "Who are you today?"

Unrealistic Expectations

Clifford: Some women are confused by what they see on television, in the streets, or what their girlfriends say.

Eric: Yea, I see that with women who read the romance novels or the less logical books.

Lawrence: A lot of women get caught up in reality TV. Some women take on the same spirit and attitudes as the reality stars. The behavior of the reality stars sometimes dictate their behavior. That behavior sometimes destroys the relationship they have. They don't realize that most of the time the stars are performing for the camera and ratings. It's not their true reality, yet they try to pattern their lives after the lives of the reality stars. That's unrealistic.

Kenneth: Women often confuse real life with what they see in movies. They take certain movies and somehow confuse them with real life relationships, and so they begin to handle their relationships with faulty logic and lies. They will take clichés and run with them. I know some women who almost always live by clichés based on no facts.

Ty: Some women always watch soap operas. If Victor cheated on his wife that day, you best believe that when some man, somewhere, gets home, his wife will accuse him of cheating. The man comes in with work clothes on and dirty from working all day. She can see that he's been at work all day, yet she accuses him of being with some other woman. It's like "I can't believe this. Is she for real?" Some women get too caught up in what's going on in the soaps and accuse their man of the doing the same things.

Kevin: I don't like it when a woman looks at her friend's relationship and tries to design her relationship like her friend's relationship. Women read magazines about this, read the stars about that, and go off on a deep end trying to make the relationship a certain way. They want their man and their homes to be like what they read about. It's dangerous when you try to make your man or the relationship like someone else's, or something you read about.

Expecting Bad

Aaron: Some women enter into relationships not expecting the best. Some women feel that if their last man did them wrong, the new man will automatically mistreat them. Even though the woman might have an interest in him, they ask their girlfriends to check him out, to see what is wrong with him, to see what he's about, and then bring them back the dirt. She should ask him whatever she wants to know. She should step to him and find out for herself if they can come together and build on something real.

Robert B.: Women allow themselves to judge the present by past experiences. If they've encountered real bad experiences in the past, they're always waiting for the past to manifest in the present. They are always expecting the past to show up.

David: Some women can't discern a good man because they're used to encountering bad men and expecting bad from every man that they meet. She then becomes afraid of repetition and sets boundaries to growing and accepting new experiences. Some women look for the bad and expect the worse.

Ryan: Women tend to be more affected by their previous relationships. If they had a bad relationship, abusive, cheating- things like that, they tend to expect that from whoever they are with next. That is very devastating to a relationship because that person who hasn't done anything wrong is going to feel like he is always being judged.

Divorce

Duncan: Some women have the baggage of divorce behind them. There is a reason why they are divorced and they have to figure out what the reason is. It could be as simple as they were just incompatible, but that in itself is a big baggage. The reason why you hear of so many people who have been married 2 and 3 times may be because they haven't figured out what the one thing is that is causing their marriages not to last. That is some baggage that they have to figure out before they could make a relationship work, or the baggage that is keeping them from bonding with the new man.

Faulty Perceptions

Julian: I think a lot of the problems that women have in relationships is based on their predicting or assuming that the relationship is going one way- when it's not. It's going another way.

Tony F: A lot of women tend to make a determination in terms of what they feel the relationship is without considering what the man's perception of the relationship is. They don't always take his perception into consideration. It causes them to foreshadow relationships before they have a chance to blossom. Once they perceive what they want it to be, or how they think the relationship should be- that's the way it's going to be. They don't take time to evaluate how the man feels about the relationship or how he perceives it should be.

Robert B.: Women give identity to the persons whom they enter into a relationship with. They tend to create in their minds a person who is or who is not. In other words, they can be with a person who everyone else sees is not correct, but in their minds they shape or mold that person into what they need and want him to be. Most men tend to look at a woman for who she is and then make a decision as to whether he can or cannot deal with her. This is a dangerous trait for women because it causes them to live in "forever hope." Forever hoping that what they actually have will become what they want or what they need.

Trust Issues

Gregory: A lot of women have a fear of trust; whether it's from what she saw daddy do to mommy or what some man has done to her. She keeps a wall up, and now, no man will be able to penetrate her wall. She's only going to give but so much. She won't let a man get inside and that keeps her from getting all that is in store for her. She could be keeping out the man she's always dreamt about, or the life she's always desired because of a lack of trust.

Greg: The trust issue. It's like, if the woman has been hurt in the past, she has the tendency to put the next guy under the microscope. The next guy after that is really under the microscope, so much so, she really drives the one after that crazy.

Childhood Influences

Aaron: Many women have a hard time communicating because, as a child, they were made to feel what they had to say was not important or wasn't understood.

Arnold: If you are raised in a household with no love outwardly expressed, you will have a very hard time showing love. You have a better chance of demonstrating love when you've had two loving parents who expressed love to and for one another.

Dominic: If your childhood environment dictated that you had to be rough, tough, defensive, and you had to fight for everything, that's going to come off in your relationship. Your language and everything you say is going to be aggressive. Who wants to be in a relationship with someone who is defensive all the time? You always have to guard and protect yourself. You are not able to be yourself. Because of the environment that some women have come out of, it's like they have no appreciation of their man, or even know the value of having a man.

Therefore, they will never be able to bond with a man.

Rick: It's all about your upbringing. You learn communication skills basically from your parents. If your mother used to control your father by hollering, screaming, and loud talking him, most likely you will do the same thing to keep your man in line. After all, when mom wanted her way, she would brow beat daddy until he would give in to her just to keep her quiet. The woman now thinks that is the way to handle or control her man.

David: Girls who are raised by their mothers will treat a man a certain way. If the father was not in the home, it is hard for the woman to adjust to the husband thing. The views that the mother had towards men and relationships will factor into the child. If the mother seeds into the child some bad ideas about men, as an adult, she will interact with her man in a negative way.

Jermaine: I work in a pretty rough area in the city. I've seen situations where a mother has three or four children by different men and the daughter has, too. It's like a family trait. I realized that a lot of things you do and how you respond to things in life are a direct result of how you were brought up, and what standards your parents set for you, especially concerning relationships. You will treat a person or allow a person to treat you in the manner in which the significant adults in your life related to each other. Whether in a positive or negative manner, you react or interact based on the behavior that was modeled for you during your formative years. Also, your childhood experiences.

Robert B.: Women look for "daddy", either a daddy who was there or who wasn't there. You can almost tell the kind of woman you are dealing with if you can understand her childhood. Women bring their childhood into present relationships and decision-making. If a woman had a good daddy, she is looking for that daddy in the man she gets with. If she had a bad daddy, she's looking for the daddy she always wanted. She will assign the man the qualities of that daddy. If she had no daddy around, she's a most vulnerable individual who starts looking for love, I feel, in too many places. In some instances, women do find their daddy and whatever daddy was doing he becomes or reflects. I am absolutely surprised at the kind of men that some women attract, and the kinds of issues they get involved with. I find that their mothers were involved with those same issues. It's really interesting how women marry the situations of their mothers. They almost recreate their mothers' lives. You may hear them say- "I'm going through the same thing my mother went through. He is just like my daddy."

The Past

Chau: A lot of women are magnets for the wrong kind of guy. Their choices cause them to enter into relationships that aren't wholesome, yet they find themselves going after the same type of men. Because they keep reinventing their past over and over again, they develop all kinds of hurts that keep them from getting too close to any man.

Julian: Sometimes women aren't open to trying new experiences. They get in a new relationship and tend to want to do the same things they did in the previous one. They don't want to explore new things or try new things. They are stuck in a rut. They want a relationship based on the past and previous experiences.

Robert C: Sometimes women assume that I'm just like the man she just got finished dealing with. Don't bring that on me. Give me a chance to mess up- if I mess up. Many of them want to revert back to what happened in the past. I don't need to know what happened in the past.

I'll find out what I need to know about you by asking you questions and us hanging out and doing things together. They are trying to create a future based on the past.

Scott: Because of past hurts, many women put up fences to protect themselves from getting hurt. When a real man comes along, he has a whole lot to contend with and to overcome. He has more to go through to gain her trust. He really has to work for it, whereas, the previous guy may not have had to work that hard. Most women encounter men who tell them how much they love them, and they're the best thing that ever happened to them, yet they have several women on the side. So, when a sincere man comes along and he tries to express himself, she usually tells him that he has not told her anything she hasn't already heard, or that she's heard that same story before. He has to now prove himself, and show her that without a shadow of a doubt, if he had the opportunity, he would love her the way that she wants and needs to be loved. He spends a lot of time trying to convince her that he is real. Because she is stuck in the past, and judging all men the same, she doesn't take him seriously.

Tony F.: Past relationships. Once an abusive relationship occurs, once a dysfunctional relationship happens, it is hard for the woman to recover. Most never recover. They carry the scars for life. They carry them into the next relationship. It may be a subconscious transference or indirect transference, but the scars are there. They are reflected in the way she presents herself to the new man. You hear it in their voices and tones. You see it in the way they perceive what you do or the type of person they think you are. It's the baggage of bringing the past tragedies, disappointments, let downs, hurts- all of that, to the relationship they are currently trying to have. A lot of women hold the crimes of the few against the many. That's rough. That's the one that gets to me the most. It is unfair to not accept me for who I am. I am not the last man, even though I may have some of his traits. I'm bringing a new person to the relationship. Stop comparing me to somebody in your past. I'm still trying to figure me out every day. I'm attempting to re-define me every day. I'm trying to put me together to present a new me to you, or a new part of me, because I am still evolving. I don't' need to be compared to the past. I realize that it's tough not to bring past experiences to a new relationship but I'm really addressing the females who tend to bring the worst with them, all the drama with them. Bringing the anger and the bitterness of the past destroys the relationship you are currently in.

"Strength and honor are her clothing."
Proverbs 31:25

Six: Woman *or* Lady?

The female is the most multifaceted person on earth. In the minds of most men, her many aspects are sometimes classified or categorized to help bring clarity or definition to her. Also, in the minds of most men, certain aspects of her revealed will define her as woman. Other aspects of her revealed will define her as lady. Here is how the men make their distinctions.

Are there any distinctions between a woman and lady?

Christopher: Woman is gender. A girl becomes a woman when she reaches the age of her menstrual cycle or the age of procreation. A lady has a strong sense of dignity. One who sits back and observes quietly. She's not loud and doesn't have to be seen everywhere and do everything. She's low keyed, quiet, reserved, a part of the group but holds on to her individuality. She is someone who doesn't give in to what a man wants, especially if it goes against her morals and ethics. She won't go against her principles just to become what the man wants.

Mamy: A lady will not accept everything a man tells her. She has her own points of view. Some women do whatever the man says to do. A lady can agree to disagree and still maintain her own individuality.

Gregory: A lady will have positive features that make her stand out, make her different from the rest of the crowd. For instance, the way she communicates. She communicates with a sense of pride. She knows who she is. It doesn't matter to her what people may think about her because she has great confidence in herself.

Trevor: A lady is one who has the utmost respect for herself. She won't put herself into disrespectful situations.

Jermaine: Yea, like open arguments.

Joseph: A lady has class. She has purpose. She has an idea of where she is going and she is on her way to getting there. A woman can be a female who is over 18, just living day by day with no real dreams or aspirations. A lady is more wary of the whims of men. A woman can be more gullible and susceptible to their games.

Richard W.: A lady is someone who doesn't accept mediocrity. She is willing to excel and go to the next level. She would have inner beauty, spiritual direction, a strong inner drive, and be self-motivated.

Gilbert: The quality of being a lady is taught, but girls grow into being women. A woman is produced by physical growth. A lady is taught to do and not to do certain things. They know how to present themselves to the world. They have presentation without being phony.

Michael R: A lady is a woman but some women can never be ladies. Respect for yourself and how you handle yourself is a difference between a lady and a woman. There are things you do and things you don't do. It's that simple. The woman who is not a lady does not know what to do, nor will she ever seek to know.

Mark: I guess there is a slight difference. A woman, more or less, is a genetic/biological description of a female. A lady would indicate that this woman has learned certain qualities and has gained certain attributes that have earned her the right to be called a lady. They've learned to conduct and handle themselves in a "ladylike" fashion.

Melvin: A woman is a generic term because any female over 18 can be considered a woman. A lady is more descriptive of how you carry yourself. A woman can be found anywhere- club, strip joint, wherever. A lady won't be found just anywhere. She is very selective about where she appears so that she won't be mistaken or misunderstood. She will conduct herself in a manner which screams-"I am a lady".

Richard C: A woman can be a person who doesn't have respect for herself and just takes what life throws at her. A lady will take life's trials and tribulations and turn a frown upside down. A lady is a leader, a woman can be a follower. A lady doesn't accept everything but a woman might go for anything. A lady is one who loves, a woman is always looking to be loved.

Ty: A woman can be someone who won't take no for an answer but will stand up and get what she wants out of life. No matter how hard it is or how many trials or tribulations she has to go through, she'll persevere through them to get what she feels life owes her.

Duane: A woman is basically a female. She may not have much respect for herself. She might exhibit behavior that is considered negative morally by society as a whole. A lady is classy. She respects herself and others. She doesn't have any negative language in her vocabulary. She's even tempered. She's someone you can take home to meet mamma.

Travis: A lady doesn't play a lot of games with people's emotions or feelings. She is very mature in the way she handles other people's emotions.

Arnold: All females grow up to be women but not all women become ladies. The difference is how she carries herself. Some women are very beautiful externally but their internal being make them ugly. They make themselves ugly by the way they act, their mannerisms, and dispositions.

Malcolm: A woman has seen, done, conquered. She is all about taking care of herself and her business.

Gerald: A lady represents maturity. She is a good mixture of strength and gentleness.

Scott: A lady is firm, strong, sensitive, caring, and loving. She knows how to get what she wants without getting into an argument with her man. She knows how to voice her opinions without yelling, screaming, without cutting off things to get her way, or to manipulate a plan.

Julian: A lady carries herself in a way that allows her to generate good feelings while in her company. She is pleasant to be around. Every little girl grows up to be a woman but not necessarily a lady. A lady is defined as having the characteristics of class and elegance. She converses well.

Michael L.: A lady has class, a woman is just female species. A lady understands what she wants and isn't afraid to say-"Hey, I am a lady. I deserve to be treated with respect. I deserve to be treated with culture. I deserve to have a car door opened for me, a chair pulled out for me, or help with putting on my jacket." It doesn't mean that she is inadequate in any way. It just means that she deserves to be protected, cared for, and nurtured. She deserves that intimacy. A woman might say-"Hey, I can do this myself. I can open my door and pull my own chair out." Even though a lady is capable of doing those things herself, she understands that they are deserving of that nurturing because of her "place". A woman hasn't necessarily come to terms with that.

Patrick: A woman may lack any expectation of courtesy extended to her, whereas a lady expects it. I think courtesy has gone by the wayside for a lot of women. They don't expect the niceties that we practiced years ago; like holding doors open for them, letting them sit on a crowded bus- things of that nature, and even using their manners: excuse me, thank you, or please. All the courtesies that we use to use, I don't see them anymore. A lot of women today have become somewhat aggressive. This you can see in supermarkets and on the road, but a lady is courteous and expects to be treated with courtesy.

Timothy: The difference is between being classy and classless. A classy woman does everything necessary to do the right thing at the right time. A classless woman will not differentiate the proper place, the proper time, the proper comment, the proper hygiene, the proper response.

Ryan: A woman is anybody who is female gender. A lady is a little more refined, classy, and has better etiquette, better manners.

Tony F: To me, a lady is someone who has the experiences that have allowed her to bring that real self to the table regardless of how a man feels about her, or how other females feel about her. A lady will have expectations for me in terms of what she perceives a real man to be. A lady brings that classiness, maturity, respect, honor, and mystique. They don't have to put everything out there. A lady can handle her business at the right time. She can voice and articulate her feelings in a mature manner.

Gerry: In my opinion, a woman is one who is

walking upright before God and herself. She knows that she has a higher calling in her life than Max Factor, Essence, Chanel, or the Nine West shoes that she is stepping out in. She sits at the table with class and indulges in intelligent conversation. She is handling her actions responsibly without faking the funk or putting on a front.

Aaron: A lady knows how to speak her mind. She has business sense and order. You know when she enters a room. She has presence about her. She's sophisticated. It's almost like-"Man, I can't touch her." She makes you want to come correct because you know that she will not accept just anything or anyone.

Robert B: A lady is one who understands propriety and appropriateness. She is more focused on "being" than what she has. She doesn't objectify herself by reducing herself to a "thing". What is important to her is the content of her character, not her make-up, clothes, and hairdo. A lady is driven by her will as opposed to her appetite. She's driven by her relationship with her Creator as opposed to what other people have created. A lady really understands that there is something bigger than what is. Her eyes are on the eternal quest, not only on the worldly quest. Because of her relationship with her Creator, she can develop the best relationships for herself because she knows her God is the best. She doesn't attract nonsense in her life. If it comes into her life, she generates a filter for it.

Lennie: A lady is gentleness. A lady demands respect by her very presence, by the way she takes care of the home, by the way her children entreat her, and by the way her husband entreats her. Even if a lady is well built, she is looked at differently. Because she is a lady and that energy is coming from her, men are not looking at her to lust but to behold her beauty. Men look at women to have sex with but men look at ladies to make love to. A man will look at a lady and just want to hold her and gently kiss her upon her brow. He's not thinking of sex, he's thinking of making love. A man will penetrate a woman before he hugs her but he will hug a lady before he penetrates her. A man will submit to a lady more than she will submit to him. A man will respond to her with humility. Ladies generate respect and a type of humbleness that make men want to protect them. She demands a type of caring and protection from a man. He knows that she is like royalty so she will allow a man to be a gentleman. A lady knows the power of silence. It's much like when Jesus was being interrogated by Pontius Pilate. His ability to be silent and follow the instructions of His Father caused Pilate to say- "I find no fault in Him." You can find no fault in a lady because her silence will speak for her. She doesn't have to defend herself. Just being who she is- just her demeanor and the way she carries herself will speak directly to all situations. Yet, a lady is someone who speaks and everyone listens- both males and females. She can walk in the room and the whole atmosphere will change. She can walk into a room of confusion and the confusion seems to diminish. It's like someone of importance just stepped in, someone of influence. A lady shows reverence for God and the law. A lady represents order.

"There is no fear in love, but perfect love casteth out fear."
I John 4:18

Seven: His Fears and Concerns

Whereas sensitivity and vulnerability are not words usually descriptive of the male persona, it is error and it is fallacy to conclude or assume that men are incapable of displaying them. For, within every relationship, there will come a time when the man must confront the issues at hand. During such times, the strength of his emotional and mental constitutions will be challenged. Even though he is determined to prevail against all odds, his perseverance sometimes brings him to the point of exhaustion. That exhaustion can breed apprehension. That apprehension may cause him to reason that his vulnerabilities are exposed, leaving his calm reserve displaced.

In the case of many men, as they attempt to regain their calm and composure, their external stances are often misinterpreted. For instance, to dispense with an appearance of weakness, they may assume postures or dispositions that to the outward eye seem insensitive or aloof. However, a closer look with the inward eye suggests they are merely trying to deflect an inner turmoil, because the sensitive heart of the inward eye knows, oftentimes, the strong exterior is a mask for the crumbling interior.

But how often have we misread or misjudged that in our men? How often have we accused them of not being as emotionally or mentally invested in the relationship as we are simply because they did not respond a particular way or react in a certain manner? Perhaps, the way they responded was the wisest way to handle the situation or concern in that moment. Also, how often have we underestimated their challenge to maintain the relationship? How often have we overlooked the fears and concerns that accompany the pressure they are under to sustain the relationship?

Again, it is of a truth that sensitivity and vulnerability are not words usually descriptive of the male persona. Once again, it is error and fallacy to assume that men are incapable of displaying them. It is even more of a truth that the same fears and concerns that women bring to relationships pervade the hearts and minds of men, also. You must know that even the best male/female relationship, at times, is most challenging.

What are the fears and concerns men have about women and relationships?

Women Will Change Up

Travis: Men fear that after they get married their wives will drastically change.

Fear of Commitment

Richard W.: Men definitely fear commitment. There are fluctuating times in a man's life. He might be at a time where he feels very strong romantically, and very positive about making the change over to marriage and spending the rest of his life with this one person, and then there are periods where he goes to the other side of the spectrum and says- "I really don't know if I can do this. I really don't know if I can deal with getting up in the morning and seeing the same person for the next 40 years." It's the commitment situation. The fear comes into play when you realize that your life is not going to be what it was in the past. The future is dictating that your life is going to be shared. Committing to sharing your life can become a fear or concern.

Kevin: Men are afraid that women will try to put them on lock down. Most men are afraid of commitment. When a man starts to give himself to a female, always in the back of his mind is, "When is she going to ask me the question?"

Joe: Men fear that women may want to commit too fast. Women have a biological clock where they want to have kids, establish a family, etc., therefore, she wants that commitment. It's the whole biological clock thing. After 30, a lot of women think they only have but so many years left to have children. That causes men to fear the pressure that women will put on them because of their own insecurities, and the timetable they've put themselves on.

Ryan: A lot of guys are very worried or fearful of getting tied down. They fear they may lose their independence. Guys are really concerned about the whole privacy issue. Nobody wants to feel like someone is constantly looking over your shoulder, that you are being judged, or accused. It makes you feel like you are being treated like a kid. It might not be the case, but it's how it feels. Some men fear that a commitment will cause them to lose their independence.

Rejection

Melvin: Rejection. Being used, or lied to.

Julian: Men fear that women will fall in love with each other and not want a man. Also, that a woman will use a man they don't love to get what she wants from him. Being used, being burnt-- whatever you want to call it.

Nayoti: Men fear giving all their trust to someone and then later finding out that they have been deceived.

Richard C.: A man fears that if a woman feeds into his ego, his dreams, and his heart, she'll stop building him up and give that attention to someone else.

Mark: If you fall in love, that person you fell in love with will no longer love you. It's hard to reconcile that.

Eric: Men fear that the whole relationship is going okay, everything is going good- then all of a sudden- it's over. If it happens enough times, it becomes a fear.

Will: One of the biggest fears or concerns of men is the fear of rejection or failure. A man might see a woman and say to himself –"Ummm, I would like to talk to this person. I kind of know this person and I know we kind of have the same values, even though she doesn't really know me." The fear of rejection or failure comes and causes a failure to act. You may let someone or something good pass by if you don't take the time to man up and go talk to this person. It's like, what have you got to lose? You don't really know this person. So what if they shoot you down? They already weren't in your life. They aren't going to be in your life any further. What are you losing? The fear of rejection or failure can really take away great opportunities for you when trying to establish a new relationship.

Made a Mistake

David: My biggest fear is having realized that I've made a mistake after I've invested years in the relationship. If you put time and work into it and it doesn't work out, it is pretty frightening to think about going out there and starting over again.

Bill: A fear or concern, especially in a committed relationship where you're not just taking a plunge into the casual is- "Is this person everything I need or want them to be? How in depth is this relationship going to go. Am I going to get all my needs fulfilled? Am I going to get everything I want?" I want the looks. I want the attraction. I want someone funny. I want someone who is interested in sports. Is it all there? Am I going to have to make some compromise or sacrifice with it? Am I making a mistake?

Fear a Setup

Ty: That a woman will try to set you up. Once she has made up her mind to have you, she will go out of her way to trap you or set you up

Rodney: Men fear that some women are gold diggers who are only out to get their money. They fear that a woman will have his baby just to keep him around.

Infidelity

Duane: Fidelity is a great issue of concern because of AIDS and various other sexually transmitted diseases.

Carroll: The ultimate— "Is someone going to replace me?" You can't get away from that. Men wish they could say that they haven't thought of that but they have. It doesn't eat them up all the time but occasionally it creeps in as a possibility. They would not want to go home one day and everything is gone because of something that wasn't talked about, or something that he totally missed. For whatever reason, they don't want to think about losing their mate to another man.

Michael L.: Men are afraid that their woman will find someone better. Someone who listens better, who is more attentive, someone who makes them laugh more, and who will give them the level of intimacy that he knows he is not giving her. Men know when they are missing the mark.

Dominic: As a man, if you are not very affectionate, or you are not very attentive to your lady, you become fearful that your actions or what you're not doing is going to cause a divide between you and your lady. For instance, let's say your wife does overtime two days out of the week. While she is doing overtime, someone is there making her laugh and giving her the attention that she is not getting at home. Those two days she is doing overtime can cause her to become more attracted to this person, and want to get to know this person that is making her laugh, taking her out to lunch, offering to pay the bill, etc. You try not to be fearful of it but you know it can happen. Once a woman decides this is what she wants to do- that's it. You can't stop her. Because it is something new, and something that she is not being offered at home, she may be tempted to try it. That's a fear when you know you aren't doing what you are supposed to be doing at home.

Her Independent Spirit

Gary: Men fear that women are going to take their jobs, make more money than they, become too independent, and leave them.

Arnold: If a woman makes real good money, has a nice career, but for some reason his career hasn't taken off, he becomes very concerned about her becoming too independent of him.

Gerry: Men fear that the woman will leave them. If she makes more money, she won't need me. If she has her own car, she won't need me.

Jesse: Some women think they don't need a man because they make $50,000 a year and their boyfriend or husband only makes $20,000. They look down on their man and become too dominant. They get promotions and forget all about him because the president of the company starts to talk to them.

Richard W.: Some men fear the over-aggressiveness of the businesswoman. They fear she may become too assertive. Women, once they become the professional, run a higher risk of divorcing, a higher risk of competing with her mate, and then the jealousy factor develops. The male feels that he's not adequate money-wise, in business or employment, to deal with a wife who is outranking him in the business world. That's something the woman definitely has to concern herself with and be careful that she's not overstepping her bounds by flaunting her position and power. She has to remember to respect her husband and the responsibilities that she took on as his woman, as his wife.

Appearing Weak

Gerry: If I don't do things her way, she's going to leave me. If I do them, she will take me as a chump.

Greg: A man fears that if he gives 100% of himself, or becomes a nice guy, the woman will take advantage of him, or take him for granted. They may give 95% and then safeguard the other 5%. That's because, as younger boys, the girls liked the boys who got the "D's" and "F's" in school. They wanted the boys who were on the corner doing this, that, and the other. The so-called "bad boys" appealed to them more. So, the nice guys, to a certain extent, finished last. They fear being too nice will make them appear as weak.

Losing Control

Kleinberg: Men fear losing themselves and losing control. Regardless of what men say, they are basically "control freaks." They also fear losing their inner child.

Timothy: Being dominated by a woman. Emotionally dominated, physically dominated, verbally dominated, or financially dominated. Not being in control. Man's biggest issue is that it is a great responsibility being head of the household, the leader, the provider, or breadwinner. Most real men want the responsibility and the accountability that comes with that. They fear not being able to do that or not being in control.

Can't Be Himself

Melvin: Not being accepted for who he is.

Tony F.: The fear of not being able to be who you are in their presence or in the relationship. You try not to be selfish. You try to cooperate to make the relationship work by giving a little here, taking a little there, just to get a balance. They fear not being accepted. They fear giving up part of who they are for the relationship.

Becoming Exposed

Robert B.: The average man fears that their pretend person will become exposed in the relationship, whereas the woman really gets to know him and his pretend person will not meet the fantasy of the woman or cannot meet the pretense.

Patrick: A man may fear that his woman might find out something about the man she doesn't like and end the relationship, or things that the man has been telling her aren't true, because men have a tendency to embellish their stories. We all try to build ourselves up. Men fear that the woman will discover the truth and will end the relationship. That can cause a lot of stress because the man is always trying to cover up who he really is.

Can't Satisfy Her

Patrick: Some women are hard to satisfy. The more you wine and dine them the more they want. She may want to travel and do other things. To accommodate her, he might get into financial difficulty because he doesn't have the money to keep her satisfied. Men also fear, as they get older, their performance in bed may not be as satisfying as once was. I think the man has to work harder than the woman. Women are usually always ready without much preparation. Men always have to go through a little bit more preparation. Because women can be satisfied more often, men can't, women can have multiples-men don't, the woman might expect more. It's easier for women to go again after the man has his moment. As men start to age, everything slows down. Their looks start to go, you gain a little weight, your face starts to undergo changes, and your stamina isn't the same. These changes have a tendency to disrupt a relationship. Also, they can cause contention because he might feel like he can't physically satisfy her anymore.

Gregory: A man sometimes fears not being able to satisfy his woman. There are so many women who are hard to satisfy. So many guys have difficulty with- "Why should I bother?" In other words, "Why should I stay here and put myself through all this havoc when she's never going to be satisfied? I can go over there and satisfy someone else." It becomes very discouraging when you have other persons on the outside-- for whatever reasons-be it deceit, or just to get over for the night- who are being supportive. Some people are just waiting to take your place and be just what the man needs. Men fear getting more support from the outside than the inside will cause them to start looking over the fence, especially if he feels that he can't satisfy his woman, anyway!

*"Do not let your heart turn aside to her ways. Do
not stray into her paths."*
Proverbs 7:25

Eight: Can't Deal With Her

The external physical beauty of a woman often
excites and entices a man. Sometimes her startling beauty
blocks his objectivity and prevents him from seeing her
for who she really is. He becomes more guided by passion
than discretion, and often ends up wasting considerable
time, effort, and money on someone who he knew was
not right for him from the beginning.

Also, there are certain types of women that shallow
men exploit and real men stay away from. Women, if you
can be characterized by the traits and actions of these
women, do not deceive yourselves. You are no more than
a temporary fling for the shallow player, and to the real
man you are only a warning sign that trouble lies ahead.

Therefore, the next question has a two-fold
purpose: to help men not compromise their time and
values to deal with *just* a pretty face and well-built body,
and to encourage women to make the personal
adjustments real men will be attracted to and would want

to deal with!

What type of women won't you deal with?
Bad Hygiene

Richard W.: I would shy away from a woman who does not practice the philosophy of cleanliness, and someone who doesn't have the graces of femininity.

Joseph: I won't deal with a woman who doesn't take care of herself. That turns me off. It doesn't matter about anything else if she's not clean. I look at a woman's hands and feet. They're the first things that I look at. If they don't look up to par, there is something wrong. To me, her hands and feet represent her.

Dominic: I can't deal with a woman who does not take care of herself. Who wants to be around a woman with bad hygiene?

Sylvester: A woman who doesn't take care of her physical and emotional well-being is a turn-off to me. If a woman, who is a little large, goes into the shower and is out in a few minutes, especially if she has some rather large body parts, can't be too clean. Bad body odor and bad hygiene is a big turn-off.

Too Dramatic

Mark: Some women have a lot of drama. Some women, through my experiences, have built up dramatic episodes in the workplace, or somewhere else- where somebody's always out to get her, or can't stand her. The whole drama aspect-- I can't deal with that.

Travis: Gossiping is probably the most offensive trait to me. I work around a lot of women and have experienced the venom of gossip. Gossip can cut you deep if you're not a strong person. A lot of things said are untrue or unfounded, but that doesn't stop some women from running with it. If you are a conscientious person, and trying to do a job well, it becomes difficult when everyone is looking at you as if what is going around is true. It's a turn-off when you're downing other people, downing your boyfriend, and downing your boss. That's a little too much negativity. I can't deal with that drama.

Ryan: Drama is worse than anything. You don't want to invite drama in your life. Some women are constantly looking for drama, arguments, or just making big statements about things. To me, that is one of the biggest turn-offs in the world. I can look past certain personality flaws, but women who are always out for attention and creating drama is just bad news. No matter how hot they are at first, it's going to get really, really old quickly, and then you are dealing with someone who is going to be creating a lot of drama for you and around you. When you try to get away from it- there's going to be more drama. That kind of attitude or persona would definitely be a deal breaker. It just gets worse. Those people are not happy. There is nothing you can bring to the relationship that will tone it down. That is just who they are. Unless you thrive on that same kind of energy, you should get away from it. It's going to eat and eat away at you. It will drive you crazy when you try to break it off with them.

Too Materialistic

Gilbert: A materialistic woman. Someone who is always, "Give me, give me, and give me." One who always has her hand out and never brings anything to the table.

Roosevelt: A materialistic woman. We begin dating- after the first couple of dates she starts asking me for money or to buy her things. I'll shy away from her. I can't deal with that.

Mistreats Others

Duncan: I can't deal with a woman who treats others like dirt. Whether it's a friend, acquaintance, or family member, if she treats them like dirt, it's an indication that she will most likely treat me the same way. If I see me not wanting to be treated how she treats others, I can't and won't deal with her.

Lack of Total Commitment

Michael L.: I never expected someone to make a lot of money, to keep the house as neat as a pin, or for me to say-"I have my half and she has her half." -things like that. Those weren't my expectations. Of course I had to be physically attracted to her, that's huge, and emotionally attracted to her, but when I got married, I had to ask myself the question-"Is this person willing, if needed, in a long term or lifetime relationship, to give up everything she is for me? Am I willing to give up everything I am for her?" Not that we have to, but we may be called to. I could get very sick or she could get very sick. Something could happen that will cause us to lose all our money in the bank, or we may have to give up all our dreams because of an unexpected misfortune. Do you love that person enough to give up everything if you had to? If you do, I think you have a committed relationship. If you don't, I think that is a deal breaker and you have to look for someone else; for that person who feels the same way about you as you do about them. There has to be total commitment on both sides. In so many relationships today, that commitment is not equal. For me- if not, it's a deal breaker. I can't deal with her!

Refuses to Change or Grow

Dominic: What would break the deal for me is if she wasn't willing to learn, but is stuck in her ways, wanting to do it her way, and won't change. I am showing her constantly that her way is not working. It's failing, yet she doesn't want to compromise or listen to what I have to offer. She won't even say- "Look, let's just try it this way." For instance, if financially she is unable to be on time with her bills, she is constantly over drafting her account and has to keep turning to me to fix what she has done, that's stressful. I know what responsibilities I have and I will take care of them. I have everything mapped out, planned out. I have everything in order, but she's living week to week, pay-check to paycheck, and is constantly coming to me to fix her finances. Every week she has a financial crisis. That's not good. That's not someone I can deal with, particularly if I offered her advice, or sat her down to show her how to handle her finances but she didn't want to take my advice or listen to me. She refuses to change. That is a deal breaker. She refuses to move forward and is living day by day. That's definitely a deal breaker.

Lack Values or Self-Worth

Richard C.: A woman who tries to get you to cater to her because of her low self-esteem. She places no or little value on herself.

Richard W.: Someone who has no gumption, no drive, who acts somewhat downtrodden. It's like she doesn't value life or herself.

Mamy: I would distance myself from a woman who doesn't share my values. If you have to think twice about why you are associating with a person, then you need to pull away from her and take your distance.

Travis: I can't deal with a loose woman. Loose in conduct and morals. Those women will keep you in constant conflict, and put you in confrontation after confrontation. I would shy away from any woman who I do not get a good feeling about. You usually know when someone is not right. If you don't get that initial good vibe, you shouldn't pursue her, no matter how fine you think she is.

Gerry: Permissiveness- what are you going to allow? Where's your line? How much can I get away with? Are my opinions leading you to compromise yourself unfavorably? If they aren't flattering to you, obviously you shouldn't do it. I can't deal with a woman who has no standards, self-respect, or self-control.

Christopher: A woman who has no class and no self-respect. She's just out there to have a good time. She's not looking for a relationship-- it's whatever, however, it doesn't matter, as long as it gets her through the moment. No challenge. I met her and I know that she is into me. I know that she likes me. She's more focused on how attractive I am and nothing else. Based on that, she is willing to sleep with me that day, that week, tomorrow. I'm in there, no challenge. It's done- no mystique. I am already in your bed. I'm already spending time with your kids and I don't even know what your hobbies are. I don't know anything about your family or background, but I know how you "want it" and when you "want it." She doesn't have morals or self-value.

James: I can't deal with an easy women. I think the chase is important. The fun is trying to get "there." It doesn't help to have someone roll over and play dead. You say come and they come. You say heel and they heel. I don't think we were made to be robotic. I think there is a certain insecurity that is exhibited when that happens. It brings devaluation to the person, because- it is true that he who stands for nothing- will fall for anything.

Tony F.: I can't deal with someone who is very indecisive. They're like, "I don't know. What do you want to do?" They never seem to make any decisions. After a while, you begin to feel that you are always asserting your wants over theirs. That is not a comfortable position for me. Also, an instant turn-off to me is a woman who lacks knowledge of self. A female who is just out there trying to be what she perceives I want. If she doesn't know who she is, she can't present herself to me. She hasn't figured out who she is. She's trying to be all my past girlfriends. She doesn't have her own value system.

Robert B.: I can't deal with a woman who defines her being by her sexuality. She is very shallow and someone who you would not want to invest in. She is a person who only sees herself as a thing. She doesn't understand the permanent nature of herself. She is like a mannequin, a dead person. She views herself as a sex object. She doesn't see herself as being intelligent. She doesn't think that she has a brain. All she thinks is that she has a body, so she dresses her body up but does nothing about her mind, and very little about her soul. She thinks that the only thing that gives her power is how she uses her body. She is a one-dimensional individual. She lacks value. That- I can't deal with!

"Rather, let it be the hidden man of the heart, with the incorruptible beauty of a gentle and quiet spirit-- which is very precious in the sight of God."
I Peter 3:4

Nine: Femininity Defined

Innate in women is the amazing ability to endure life's hardships. Much too often, to overcome unfortunate circumstances allotted to her by life, she is forced to draw deep within to extract the strength to persevere. However, when unfortunate circumstances persist too frequently, she will tire from always having to expose herself to the challenges constantly threatening her. Therefore, in order to sustain and preserve herself, she may feel compelled to shield or guard herself, or emerge into another self to protect the real self.

For example, a lot of women have become hardened and embittered by the exploitation of the counterfeit men they've allowed in their lives. Many have vowed that no man will ever use or abuse them again! Consequently, many of them have assumed cold and callous postures to protect their damaged emotions. This posture has caused some of them to abandon their femininity, or project an image of which some might consider as borderline masculinity. This posture has not only alienated the affections of the current man in their lives but has repulsed men in general.

To those women-- whether your hardness is a direct result of life's victimization, or a result of your bad choices and experiences with counterfeit men- you can recover or rediscover the feminine nature that allows the warm and adorable you!

To encourage the rediscovery process- please consider what "real men" have to say regarding femininity.

How do you define femininity?

Daryl: The ability to be soft and sensitive, a gentle spirit, an easy-going personality, and pleasant demeanor. Gentleness and tenderness has a lot to do with my definition of femininity.

Jermaine H: Tenderness, someone who is gentle. I think of the word "ladylike". How you feel about yourself and how you carry yourself reflects what or how you feel about your femininity.

Leroy: Femininity is a delicate graceful demeanor, soft to the touch. She is a woman who carries herself in such a way that you can differentiate her from her surroundings. She exudes an element of mystery.

Mark: Femininity is an inner sense. It's something a woman should exude. You don't have to portray yourself as being as rough and tough as the guys but you can be just as good.

Richard C: She walks around but not to "shake it fast" or to show people what she's working with. A feminine woman is emotional but she knows when it is expedient to be emotional and when it isn't appropriate to be emotional.

Reuben: Some women have a calm about themselves. No matter what goes on around them, they maintain a certain calm. They'll get upset but won't let whatever is going on around them provoke a negative response in them. They'll maintain control. I think femininity is how calm you are when your storm arises. How well you handle your storms.

Gregory: From a physical standpoint, she can be firm, yet soft. From an intellectual standpoint, she can be smart, but maneuver in a sense that if she is more educated than I am, she is smart enough to make me feel good about where I am. From a personal standpoint- I don't mean to use this storybook kind of description, but it's almost like she is a queen. She carries herself in a queenly manner. She's got class and feels good about herself. She knows that she is somebody.

Timothy: The first thing that comes to my mind is cleanliness. Healthy hygiene and personal cleanliness is the best expression of femininity to me.

Joseph: A woman who can throw it on. I know when I go out, I'm sho'nuff stepping. I like a woman who can step with me. I like the matching pocketbook and shoes. Femininity to me is a woman who can sho'nuff dress. She is versatile with her attire. You can come at me with jeans and some sneakers- whatever - just as long as you know how to throw it on- I'm content!

Bill: To me, femininity can be a woman's physical shape and looks. It's what makes her a woman: her curves, her hairstyle, or how she applies her makeup.

Duncan: A feminine woman is one who is fixed up. She likes to look good. She doesn't dress up differently to go to work as opposed to just being home, or out with her husband. She feels good about herself and it reflects in the way she dresses, looks, and how she carries herself.

Dominic: A woman displays her femininity in different ways: her walk, her talk, and her actions. Also, the way she attends to you, and is affectionate towards you expresses her femininity. Femininity is also an attitude. A woman can have on sneakers, jeans and a t-shirt, yet be very feminine, sensual, and very attractive because of the aura or vibe she's presenting. Another woman can have all the looks, have on a beautiful gown, nice outfit, yet be the most unattractive, loud, and rude person. Femininity is all about the attitude and the vibe you are presenting.

Patrick: You can have a woman who, according to others, may not have a lot of looks going on but dresses the right way, puts her hair the right way, holds herself up, and walks a certain way- that woman is feminine. She makes you look and notice her. You can have a woman who is good-looking but doesn't hold herself up, who doesn't know how to walk, who doesn't know how to talk, and you look and say-"She has the looks but she has no femininity." I think femininity has a lot to do with how you approach people and the way you present yourself. A feminine woman takes care of herself, has good self-esteem, and presents herself a certain way.

Tony F.: Captivating and alluring. I think of powder- the scent of a woman, delicate, fragile, beauty. I think of the way they walk, the way they carry themselves and present themselves to the world, as well as me.

Trevor: The exact opposite of masculinity. Femininity suggests a certain softness and sensitivity of nature. It can be expressed in her scent- how good she smells, as well as the way she walks.

Jermaine: Oh yes! Definitely the way she moves- the motion of her body.

Trevor: A feminine person exudes womanliness.

She radiates femaleness. It's like, if your eyes are closed and a feminine woman walks by, you'd know it was a woman who just passed by.

Malcolm: A woman's walk, her sensuality, her style. There are so many things that can bring her femininity to the forefront. A feminine woman has a style like "Art." If she carries herself well and keeps up her hygiene, she is like a piece of Fine Art.

Carroll: A feminine woman is soft, nurturing, understanding, caring, supportive, compassionate, and sensitive.

Roosevelt: The way she moves, the way she talks, the type of clothing she wears that compliments her shape and personality. It's the different styles of her hair-whether short or long. The way she smells. There is nothing like a good smelling woman. Make-up and all the accessories make me find you feminine but they are just additions to what you're already putting out there.

Ryan: Femininity to me is that nurturing mentality, the softer personality and physicality. It's also being comfortable with being a woman and owning that. It's about finding yourself and being who you are.

Kevin: Chasteness in dress, attire, appearance, and mannerisms. These are the things that are appealing to me. It doesn't matter what day of the week it is, what the occasion is, or what the reason is - the woman always fits the moment!

"If it is possible, as much as depends on you, live peaceably with all men."
Romans 12:18

Ten: Just to Get Along With Her

In a good relationship, there must be a mutual exchanging of thoughts, ideas, goals, expectations, but-more importantly, a mutual exchanging of self. However, many relationships are unbalanced because one person usually has the burden of doing more than the other to sustain the relationship. Consequently, the one who feels he is contributing more frequently often becomes frustrated, especially if he assumes the other person has adopted a cavalier attitude towards the relationship. However frustrated, he must guard against becoming overly critical and fault-finding, because even though there is a degree of legitimacy to his concerns, we know that frustration and dissatisfaction often exaggerate a situation.

Therefore, compromise and concession become essential components to gaining or restoring a harmonious relationship. But once a determination is made on each part to get the relationship back to a peaceful flow- the struggle then becomes-- who will concede first.

However, the scripture quoted above gives accountability to both partners to make peace and pursue it throughout the relationship. Here is how the men feel they make their peace.

What is the one thing men do just to get along with women?

Wait It Out

Clifford: Sometimes, you just have to wait things out because you've either said or done the wrong thing. Just wait things out or until they blow over.

Apologize

Brian: Smile, nod, and apologize.

Talk

Greg: Talking at times when the man doesn't feel like talking. A man doesn't always feel like talking.

Surrender

Gilbert: When you're right, act like you're wrong for the sake of argument.

Gary: Say, "Yes! I agree with you!"

Lennie: Surrender! Just totally surrender. Some women need for you to just surrender. They need the white flag drawn and they need for you to say, "I surrender to you!"

Share

Kleinberg: Get it in your head that the single life is over. Come to terms with the fact that this is what you wanted. It takes hard work. This may be the hardest thing you've done in your life but it's the most rewarding thing.

Aaron: In order to maintain peace in the house, you have to share your space and time. You have to compromise space and time.

Let Her Have the Last Word

Roosevelt: She's always right. She's got to be right. She has to have the last word.

Daryl: Let them have the last word, especially if she's in a bad mood and is really giving it to you. It's easy to retaliate with some of the things that women come out with. They can be kind of degrading but you just have to let it go, humble yourself, and don't take it to the point where there has to be a winner, even though the choice of her words and how she says them can really demean a man.

Rodney: A man has to be very apprehensive and reserved about how he discusses certain issues. He cannot always feel that he has to have the last word. Sometimes, he has to say, "Alright, I'm just going be quiet on this and talk about it at a later time so that things won't escalate into an argument." You can be having a little debate and it can escalate into an argument. So, you might have to let the discussion go and just say, "Alright, okay." Later, at a cool point, you can say, "Hey, remember what we were talking about . . .?"

Shut Up

Christopher: Shut up and give them what they want. If you don't, they will go on and on and on and on and on! Just be quiet and go along with the program.

Jermaine H.: Sometimes men just need to shut up. At times, I'm trying to interject, give my opinion, and trying to solve everything. Sometimes, you just need to listen and shut up.

Gerry: Shut up! You have to shut up! Men look at things differently. Sometimes, they have a tendency to be too vocal of their likes, dislikes, and opinions. Because men think and feel differently than women, they have to shut up and really pay attention.

Just Listen

Tony F.: Listen. Just listen. Let them talk. Just let them talk, every once in a while, throw in an "Uh-huh, alright." Listen to what they're saying. Somewhere, in that hour or two of conversation, you might get an idea of what she really wants to talk to you about. Just shut up and listen.

Leroy: You have to learn when to turn on the listening ear and when to turn up the mouthpiece. If you don't, she will go on and on and on. Know when to listen and when to respond. Know when they want a response. Most of the time, you can't say anything at all. Just sit there and listen.

Pretend to Listen

Will: Pretend you are listening. Every once in a while, say- "Ummm, yea!"

Let Her Be Right

David: Letting the woman feel that she is right and has won the argument-- even though you know that you are right- beyond a shadow of a doubt. You realize that it's more stress being caused by arguing so you let it go. Then you get peace in the house and the woman is happy.

Do What She Wants

Kevin: Men feel that they have to conform. They feel they have to be exactly what it is that she wants him to be, or do exactly what she wants him to do.

Travis: At some point, just do whatever they say so you won't have to hear the constant nagging. Men sometimes give in because they do not like to do a lot of arguing. We find ourselves doing things just for the sake of peace. It really becomes a problem when women realize that, and try to manipulate a situation to go their way because they know we don't like confusion and arguing.

Jermaine T.: Just say, "Okay baby, okay baby! Yeah, baby! If that's what you want, that's how it's going to be. Okay, baby!"

Shop

Gregory: Going shopping. I don't like to shop. But she wants me to take her to 20 different stores and wind up going back to the first store we started out in to get what she should have gotten in the first place. Let's find a happy median, if I go with you, let's understand before we go that we're not going to 20 stores. Let's kind of have some idea of what you want before we start out, then I won't get uptight with you and you won't get uptight with me for not wanting to go with you. Let's have an understanding from the outset.

Julian: Oh my gosh! What is the one thing that men have to do just to get along with women? From my point of view- there is no one thing! There are some things! You have to take the trash out, put the seat down, vacuum every once in a while, cook every once in a while, change the diapers, take the kids to school, take care of the kids, every once in a while- plan vacations, plan for dinner, go to the movies, you have to walk the dog, walk the cat, bring her gifts, buy her diamond rings, buy her more diamonds, you have to go shopping with her, sit there while she goes through some unrealistic bizarre fantasy of a shoe search, let her go through about 20 pairs of shoes when she can just pick one and leave, but you have to stay four hours which is totally ridiculous to a man. It's just so many things. Men just don't understand that women like to shop. Men are looking for the nearest chair until they can leave to go home. You can't sum it up as just one thing. There are so many things men have to do in a relationship. My answer to that one thing is- "There is no one thing!"

"Wisdom is the principal thing-- therefore, in all your getting, get understanding."
Proverbs 4:7

Eleven: Accepting the Man

At different stages of life, in various aspects of our lives, we all will come under the careful scrutiny of others. There will be instances where the discerning eyes are blinded by false interpretations of who we really are.

In those instances, the faulty perceptions, more often than not, will subject us to misunderstandings and misrepresentations, causing feeble attempts to be made toward our transformation. As such attempts are made, almost always, feelings of rejection begin to surface. If the feeble attempts persist too frequently, over the course of time, those feelings of rejection will cause us to shut down, or shut out those persons whom we feel have never, nor will ever, accept us for who we really are.

Therefore, we should never be blinded by personal preferences or skewed perceptions of who we want a person to be. Nor should we become misguided by the unrealistic expectations we place upon a person to become who we think he should be, *because-* we are who we are! Sometimes our different forms of expressions may allow *variations of, or deviations from ourselves,* but rest assured--we will eventually retreat back to who we really are-- *and,* if there is no careful vigilance given to maintaining an awareness, acceptance, and allowance of one's "real" or "true self", there will always be the tendency to conjure up false conceptions of who we think the other person really is, and expectations placed on him to reflect who he could never -nor should ever –become!

What is the hardest thing for women to accept or understand about a man?

Men Want to Be Faithful

Daryl: A typical married man-- I'm thinking about a Christian man-- wants to be faithful to his wife. He doesn't want anyone else and wants his relationship to have a certain level of romance in it. Of course sex factors in with that. They want to love their wives totally and completely, and when a woman isn't compliant in that area on a regular basis, or they get to the point where they reject the man often, it does something psychologically to a man that is very demeaning, and just not good for the relationship. It can put the man in an uncomfortable situation of compromise.

Victims of Upbringing

Arnold: It may seem simple or clichéd, however, a lot of women need to really accept that men are the way they are because of how they were raised.

Not All Men Are Sex-Graved

Malcolm: It's hard for a woman to understand that a man doesn't have to sleep with every woman he knows, or every woman he comes in contact with.

Julian: Not all men are dogs. Not all men want you for your body or sex. Some men actually want relationships, marriage, and children. There are men who will accept women with children because they realize that they're in the same situation that they are in-- just trying to find someone to love and be loved by. Sex is not the only thing on their minds.

Men Don't Need Changing

Daryl: Some women don't understand that if you try to change a man to what you want him to be, you will detract from the relationship. They have a hard time accepting him for who he is, therefore, she tries to make him dress the way she wants him to dress, and tries to make him act the way she wants him to act. It's hard for women to accept the fact that she cannot change a man or that he does not need changing.

Travis: It is so hard for a lot of women to understand that men don't need changing, but a lot of them feel that need to change you in some way, shape, or form. They don't understand that most men are secure in who they are, and when women try to alter them, it produces conflict. Most men feel as though they've successfully existed before the significant other appeared, happily embraced the single life, so there shouldn't be an issue of trying to change them. After all, they were good enough to attract them.

Kenneth: The man needs for his woman to understand and accept him more than trying to change him. If you met someone who interests you, or someone who you want to get to know better to develop a relationship with, why would you want to change them? No longer would they be the person who intrigued you in the first place. We all grow in what we do or feel. It's a dynamic process-- or it should be. So, if we're going to grow, it's good to grow together. If you don't grow together, you will grow apart. The man needs for his woman to be practical and understand that it is his job to correct or change himself. If you think you can change someone by manipulation, by psychological gamesmanship, by emotional gamesmanship, by emotional blackmail-- you're totally fooling yourself. It's a mistake to try to change someone because you would rather have things this way or that. Woman would go farther if they learn to understand and accept their man a little more graciously, and not constantly try to change him.

Will: I find that a lot of women are always trying to change their man. Whether it's a hobby, his habits, or his daily routine, they always seem to try to change the man in some capacity. Suppose they don't want to change? I've had people in my past who tried to change certain things or beliefs about me that I just didn't want to change. You shouldn't have to change for someone. When you get into a relationship with someone, they should accept you and like for you, for you being you. You shouldn't have to change. If there are some small things that need adjusting, and if the change is for a good reason, then it's okay to change. But trying to change someone into a completely different person, I feel, is sick. Why did you even get into a relationship with this person in the first place?

Men Want Women to Initiate Sometimes

Julian: If a man feels that he is initiating all the time, he gets bored and tired. Men love women who initiate. Very few men would turn women down as far as talking, affection, caring, understanding- all that. A woman who does not initiate ruins her selection of men because most of the good men, for whatever reason, don't initiate. They feel as if they don't have to, especially if they have high standards. The reason why men don't initiate is because women control the rejection thing. Men don't like to be rejected. If a man feels that a woman is going to reject him, he won't initiate anything. It really makes sense. Women have been taught as they grew up that men are supposed to initiate *everything*. I don't think it is totally true because men, nowadays, are not doing it. Usually the ones who initiate are the ones who don't have a lot going for themselves. They are the ones who get the women. The men who are waiting for true genuine women are going to be very selective. They may feel the woman won't initiate because there is no interest.

Gregory: A man can be turned off by always having to be the aggressor or initiator. It is like- what the heck- is she ever motivated or stimulated? It can make him feel like he is begging.

A Man's Humanity

Gregory: It's hard for women to understand a man's humanity. A man is simply a human being, nothing more. He struggles with whatever he is trying to achieve. If he fails, he does not need to be beat up on. Men beat up on themselves enough. Recovery takes time. It doesn't take much for a person to relapse, therefore, if he is trying to recover from a mistake he's made, he doesn't need his woman to keep reminding him that he's made that mistake. One of the worst things women can do when there is a disagreement, is to always remind him of what he did in the past. To go down the line to bring up as many things as she can possibly dig up, even though it is 10 years later. That can be very damaging to a man.

Patrick: It's hard for some women to accept or understand that a man is human and will make mistakes. He doesn't need for you to hold it over his head. Some women never seem to forget any type of indiscretion that a man made, even if it happened in the past. They seem to bring it up constantly.

Dominic: It's hard for some women to accept that a man is human and doesn't have all the answers. A lot of men, particularly today, don't have fathers in their lives. Myself, I don't know all the answers. I am still learning and experiencing life. When I encounter a problem with my sons, and I have no experience with it, I do think back and say-"Wow, I wish I had a father to call or someone I can call." I wish I had someone in my life to mentor me and guide me, or someone to whom I can say-"Hey, this is what's going on. This is what I got." I don't have that. It gets tough sometimes but you have to work through it. I have co-workers and older guys who I might bring up a situation with them to see what their response is, however, it's hard for some women to understand that a man is only human, that he struggles with certain issues, therefore, he may need help in certain areas.

A Man Will Be a Man

Tony F.: That man— each individual man-- is going to be who he is. No matter what she does, what games she plays, how she tricks him, how she captures him, he's going to be who he is. His real self will show up. A lot of women won't accept that.

Robert B.: It's hard for women to accept that a man is just a man. You have to understand that he will be a man, and that you have to know the person who stands before you. You have to get to know that person and accept that he is who he is, nothing more.

He Knows What He Wants

Patrick: In a lot of cases, a can man sit down and discuss his needs with his woman and it still doesn't happen. The connection is not there. It doesn't seem to register that he knows what he wants. It's like a gap between that man and woman and she just can't understand or figure what he wants or needs, even though he discussed it with her.

Julian: Some women are in relationships and have no idea what their man wants. They have a hard time trying to understand what he wants. They have a hard time believing that he knows what he wants. Men, in general, really want relationships but a relationship where the woman is playing games, not really remembering things that her man says, or what he wants, can really have a negative impact on his feelings for her.

Ty: It's hard for women to really understand or accept what a man really wants and how to assist him in getting to where he desires to be. Also, it's hard for women to accept or understand that a man even knows what he wants.

Timothy: Women assume they know what a man wants without even consulting with him about his wants or needs. Even when he communicates what he wants, sometimes the woman may not believe that is what he wants. She sometimes feels that he doesn't really know what he wants. He's giving out clues and signals about what he wants but she doesn't take him seriously. She takes him for granted. After he gets tired of trying to convince her that he knows what he wants or needs, and seeks it from someone else, then she becomes mad. Mad at him, mad at the girl, mad at his family, if he has a son that looks like him, she becomes mad at him. She's shocked and mad, yet she still hasn't realized that he was trying to communicate what he wants, his own way, the whole time, but she acted like she was clueless or didn't believe him.

A Man's Sensitivity

Rodney: It is hard for some women to accept that men can be sensitive or affected by what goes on around him. On a daily basis, a man experiences ups and downs that may cause him to display some type of sensitivity or vulnerability. Every day will not make him feel optimistic and she needs to encourage him. She needs to limit her criticisms when she finds that he is going through a sensitive and vulnerable time.

Michael W.: Just because men are nowhere near as overt as women are in showing or expressing their feelings and emotions does not, in any way, mean that we do not have as much love and affection as they have for the relationship. Women are naturally more expressive and verbal about their feelings.

Kenneth: It's hard for women to accept that men can hurt and do hurt. They can hurt very deeply over things that you may not think hurts them. Men don't always show their hurt. They try to diminish the significance of the hurt. Men basically have fragile egos.

Joseph: Men are just as sensitive as women are. We have emotions. Some of us might act like we have hard coated shells around us, like we're "hardcore", but we are sensitive. It's just that some of us are dealing with hurt and we may not know how to show our emotional side.

Men Can Be Truthful

Hooper: Some women cannot accept that a man can be real about his affections, his devotion to her, and that he can be kind, understanding, and truthful. They keep looking for his faults or his downfalls.

Gilbert: It's hard for women to accept that men can be honest and sincere, and that all his actions aren't done with ulterior motives.

Mark: Men can be truthful. If he says that he loves you, 9 out of 10 times, he means it. If a man says that he feels that way about you, 9 times out of 10, he feels that way. Men really will be truthful with you.

Kleinberg: It's hard for a woman to accept or understand that a man can be sincere when he wants to patch things up after he's messed up. They sometimes don't accept the apology because they don't believe he's going to change.

Jesse: It is hard for women to accept that men are truthful. They always doubt your honesty and sincerity and they seem to be more willing to accept a lie rather than the truth.

Men Will Look

Larry: We like to look at women. Ninety-nine percent of the time it doesn't mean anything. It doesn't mean that we're looking at another woman to replace them. It doesn't mean that we're going to pursue. It doesn't mean any of that! It simply means- "Man, look at that!" That's all it means. You are a wonderful creation and we love the way you look!

Jermaine H.: It's hard for women to understand our physical nature and how we like to look at women. We are going to look. Regardless of what you wear or what you don't wear, men are going to look. Men will look-- point blank! Married or not. It's just how men are wired.

Patrick: Men have a tendency to look at other women. His woman is wondering if he sees something in another woman that he doesn't see in her. It doesn't mean that he will go after her, or even wants her. Men just like to look.

Ryan: Men are going to look at other women. There's absolutely no getting around that. It doesn't, in any way, take away from his woman or how he feels about her. No matter how involved with his woman he is, he's going to look at other women. He may not be trying to do anything with them, but he's going to look. It's not personal. A lot of feelings get hurt over something that should not hurt anybody. Men don't mean for it to be insulting. It's a matter of physicality, how we are wired.

Leroy: It is hard for most women to accept that a man will be a man. There are certain things that he will do because he is wired that way. A man, every once in a while, even if he is with his wife, will look at another woman. I don't know that women should necessarily accept that but they definitely shouldn't be insecure about it. Many think that they are seeing something in them that they don't see in their wives but that is not always true. That's just our wiring. It shouldn't be a normal practice, but every once in a while, a man will glance at another woman.

Don't Like to Be Compared to

Dominic: A lot of times, particularly when you are just starting out in a relationship, you don't know where you can and cannot step. You have to be careful as to what you say and what you do. In your mind, you already know where the line is and when someone crosses that line, it's going to upset you. It's going to cause some type of friction. But if you are just starting out in a relationship and some lines are crossed, you never want to be compared to the woman's previous experience or previous man. You never want to be referenced with someone else's situation, whereas the woman might say- "Well the last time- so and so did this." Who wants to hear that? You never want to be looked as less than her prior man. At least give your man a chance to step up and do whatever it is you want him to do, or the task you put before him without comparing him to the last man. It's hard for a lot of women to understand that they should not compare the new man to the ex, or the new relationship to the prior one.

Need Space

Greg: In a married relationship, men still have a need to be who they are. He still needs to have his own personality intact. He needs some sense of independence, be it a room or closet-- his own personal space. He needs a safe haven where he can go to meditate when things get tough. It's not a knock against the marriage. In a marriage, you have to be a couple but the wife needs to be who she is and the man needs to be who he is. That shouldn't be considered an attack against the marriage, nor should it put the relationship in danger.

Roosevelt: We need our space. When I say we need our space, I'm not saying to be absent from the relationship. I just might need to bond with my male friends or just be to myself. Every now and then, we need our space.

Larry: I wish that women would understand that sometimes we don't want to be around them. We just can't. We would go crazy if we were around them all the time. They have to let us sometimes do what we want to do and not put the guilt trip on us. We need space and time.

Julian: There are some things that men like to do where they just want to be left alone. Watching football, basketball, or other sports are some of those things. Do a lot of women understand that? No!

Nayoti: You need time alone to work out problems, or to mentally figure out how to make the relationship better.

Joe: It's hard for women to understand that just because a man likes to go out and have fun does not mean that he doesn't care. He may decide that he wants to hang out on a Saturday with friends to watch a football game. It doesn't mean that he doesn't care about his family. It doesn't mean that he does not want to be around them.

It's just that he sometimes wants space to do other things.

Will: Men really do need their space. You need space apart from one another for personal reflection, a hobby, or whatever it is you like to do. You need a little distance from time to time. Just a little bit, not a whole lot. It can actually help the relationship out.

Let Him Walk Away

Ronald: Some women don't understand that when you get into an argument and the guy turns around and walks away, you have to let him walk away. He'll come back later and talk about it. It is hard for women to let him walk away. If he doesn't, he's going to end up saying something that he means but will come out the wrong way. He needs to leave to clear his head.

Aaron: There are times when a man needs to be by himself to organize, reevaluate his life, and replenish himself on his own, outside of her and the relationship. He needs to go. Women don't understand that. They feel as though we don't love them, we're turning our backs on them, and we're leaving and not coming back. "I don't believe he did this to me. Why did he leave me?" You two can be arguing and she'll want a response right then. He may not have an answer for you right then. He may need to leave out to think some things through. When he comes back, he'll be better able to communicate with you. He'll be more settled. Two hot heads won't be able to resolve anything. Let him walk away. He needs air. He needs space and time apart so that he can better articulate how he really feels after he's gotten a chance to think things through. You have to let him leave out.

Men Think and Communicate Differently

Mamy: It is hard for some women to accept that husbands and wives will have different opinions and points of view on certain issues. Instead of trying to persuade him to her way of thinking, she should accept his points of view and try to learn from them.

Julian: It's hard to get into women's heads that men express their feelings differently than women do. Women are so used to saying, "I would do this or I would do that." because they're not men. Until a woman tries to understand the man she wants, tries to understand how he behaves, she'll always be wondering- "How can I get him to do that." You're never going to get him to do t*hat* because you don't understand him. Men approach things differently. It's hard for women to understand that we think and communicate differently than they do.

Gerry: How we think- the processing of information for us is very different than it is for women.

Robert B.: A lot of women do not have an understanding of the male persona. We are different in terms of how we process, how we hear each other, and sometimes that is where the confusion lies.

Greg: When a man is silent, it doesn't mean that he doesn't care. Sometimes men are quiet because they're thinking about a particular thing. Men won't just say things without giving some thought and consideration to what they want to say. He may be pondering what to say and might not want to discuss what he's feeling when the woman wants to discuss it. He might talk about it 10 minutes later, hours later, or the next day. Men are forced on a consistent basis to discuss certain things they don't feel like discussing at the time. I think a lot of women see that as him not caring about what she's going through. It's just that he doesn't feel like dealing with it right then. If you back him into a corner, he'll end up saying something that he will regret. If you give him time to think about what he wants to say, you might get a better response. Men and women are not on the same timetable.

Timothy: It is hard for women to understand that the average man is a poor communicator. No matter what they feel or say, the average man needs more time and space to communicate regardless of the level or content of conversation. It's all about timing. When trying to have a conversation about very important issues, there needs to be a mutual understanding about the timing of the conversation. The timing has to be agreed upon. The lack of proper timing is what spurs most true arguments. It goes back to men not being easily able to cycle our emotions and women being more self-serving. Women tend to be more ready, more willing, or more eager to get things said, and the pressure they put on the men to respond is one of the things that deter men from dealing with any emotions at all. Most men need more time to allow things to register so they won't respond in a derogatory or abusive manner, or be in rebuttal strictly from emotion, with no real thought. The pressure to respond immediately- the average man will avoid, disregard, and allow the buildup of wrong emotions until every little thing becomes a big thing and the big things become that much harder to deal with. So, at times, the woman just needs to realize that her man needs a few minutes to get himself and his thoughts together, and not pressure him for an immediate response that will only lead to miscommunication.

"Let each of you look out not only for his own interests, but also for the interests of others."
Philippians 2:4

Twelve: The Needs of a Man

The resilience of men is remarkable! Their recovery is impressive! From all external indications, they are back on top again! They speak to their adversary that sought to subdue them, and command him to make reciprocity. Now, we look upon them in wonder and bestow upon them accolades and honor-- *but* our ears may deaf to the cry of their soul-- the cry of a bruised and wounded soldier!

Most of us would agree that there is an all-out attack on marriages. What's propagated in the media is a sad commentary on how marriage is regarded today. With the flagrant glorification of infidelity, and the whole sex propaganda, the sanctity of marriage is often discounted. Because of this, not only do we have to contend with the internal intricacies of the relationship, but we have to fight against the external influences and distractions that intensify the battle to keep the relationship going, growing, and flowing.

So, as your man fights against the outside forces that try to destroy the relationship, become to him a discerning eye, because- no matter the strengths, no matter the capabilities, humanity dictates that each time a person enters into battle he loses a little of himself. Whether his expenditures are of his mental or physical energies, he loses a little of himself. Then it becomes your responsibility to assess the loss so that you can present yourself as his healing balm.

Therefore, it would behoove you to remain tuned to your man. He may have won the outward battle, but inwardly he may be crying out to you to soothe a hurt *or* **meet a need!**

Are women in tune with the needs of their men, and what are some needs men have?

A Sense of Togetherness

Sylvester: A man needs to feel a strong sense of togetherness with his woman. He needs to feel that they are growing together instead of drifting apart. Togetherness creates a better environment for all. Togetherness keeps the relationship strong. It allows you to communicate without saying words.

Encouragement

Kevin: Men need support, understanding, and encouragement.

Arnold: A man needs a woman who will encourage him to do better in some way, shape, or form. He needs someone whom he can trust wholeheartedly to keep him encouraged.

Gerald: Men need a lot of encouraging. We get beat up a lot. We are denied a lot of things that are offered to our counterparts and not to us. We need to be encouraged to hang in there.

Patrick: Women, at times, can put a man down. Men need to be built up and encouraged. Some women always expect men to give them compliments but they don't like to give compliments. A man needs a woman who understands his need for encouragement and compliments and not deny him of those needs, or manipulate them if he is in an argument or disagreement with her.

Appreciation

Gerry: A man needs immediate reciprocal appreciation. When you see that he's making progress, let him know that you appreciate it so that he'll want to do it again.

Aaron: A man needs to be complimented or thanked when he does things. When you ask him to do something, don't be too demanding, let him know that you appreciate him helping out.

Ryan: Men like to feel appreciation. When they don't feel that, they wonder why they are doing what they're doing. Everyone wants to feel wanted and appreciation. Everyone wants to feel that the other person appreciates what you are doing for them. They want to feel like the other person appreciates you being there and if it's not expressed, there will be a breakdown.

Friendship

Christopher: Men need friendship. Women need to spend time, even before building an intimate sexual relationship, trying to become his friend. They need to build a friendship. Be my friend, be my confidant. Confide in me, talk to me. Friendship is the foundation of any relationship.

Ronald: A man needs companionship from his wife. He needs to be friends with her.

Michael: You need someone for companionship.

Someone who's going to be your back and you'll be hers. Someone you can tell your story to and she knows she can tell her story to you. She is your best friend.

Nayoti: A man needs friendship from his mate. He needs for her to be a true friend.

Support

Roosevelt: Men need support. When you love somebody, no matter what you say, whatever that person thinks about you is very important. Whenever you set your mind to do something, you're going to want the support of your loved one. Just the support of saying "Yeah, I might not agree with what you're doing but you're doing something positive to try to make things better. I support you." Verbally express your support.

Nayoti: He needs support. Stand by your man, even if you feel he's not right. You can give your input but stand by him. Some people have to learn from their mistakes. If it's a mistake that is not drastic to the relationship or your well-being, show your support by standing by him. He needs your support.

Bill: Men need support. They need to know the person they are in a relationship with has their back and is going to support them, wrong decision or right.

Greg: A man needs a shoulder to lean on for support. For instance, if a man and his woman are in a conversation and she thinks her man is wrong, and someone else thinks her man is wrong, she supports him in front of that person but when she gets him home, she lets him know that he was wrong, yet she still supported him.

Kleinberg: Men need emotional support and agreement support. For instance, whatever you decide that you are not going to do, like arguing in front of friends, in front of the children, or not going to bed angry, whatever it is that you've decided-- stick to it. Support him. Whenever you have your issues- discuss them. Whatever you set out to do, it is necessary to be in agreement. Support each other.

To Be Tuned to Him

Michael W.: Some women downplay the amount of tension and stress that men incur from being in the workplace all day. They should be more in tune with what he has to go through and how it affects him.

Michael B.: A man needs his woman to listen a little more to what he wants, ask him what he wants, know what he wants, and understand what he wants. That's how you become in tune with your man.

Hooper: He needs for his woman to be sympathetic to all the things that he is going through. She should be in tune with that.

Roosevelt: I feel that you have to be in tune with the person you're in a relationship with. A lot of times, a person won't just come out and say, "I'm sad today, I don't feel good today", or "I'm not in the best of moods." She should be able to see that, to read that in her man. She can then go to him and treat him accordingly. She should be able to recognize that he's feeling a little down. The man needs for his woman to be in tune with him so that she can read his moods.

Timothy: A man needs for his woman to be tuned to what he is going through. If a man comes home, goes to his corner, sits and stares at the walls, it should be obvious that something is going on inside of him. She needs to discern his mood. He might just want for you to say, "Look, baby, I'm going to leave you alone. I see that something is troubling you. If you need me, I'll be in the other room." Or, he may need for you to say- "Hey, baby, I see you had a hard day, I'm taking you out." You have to learn how to discern your man. It takes time for some men to make the transition of coming from the workplace into the home. He needs his downtime to readjust. If she insists on involving him in a discussion as soon as he gets in the door, it will create a problem. He feels that she has been thinking about what she wants to say all day, and now she wants an immediate response from him. He needs a minute to take in what she is saying. He's not trying to be disagreeable, but she needs to realize what kind of a day he's had, and if he responds the wrong way, she shouldn't accuse him of not wanting to talk to her. It's not that. It's just that he needs a minute to get in the house and relax. She should be in tune with her man to know his moods.

To Be Needed

Greg: A man wants a woman who can be independent, yet makes him feel that he's needed, that she needs him in her life.

Robert C.: Make me feel like I'm wanted but don't make me feel wanted by using me as a puppet. Men can tell the difference. I love to feel like I'm needed.

Bill: Men instinctively need to be needed. They need to feel they are still the strongest in the family, that they can protect the family. They need to have a sense of need.

Honesty

Greg: He needs someone who will have his back, yet be truthful.

Gerry: Men also need honesty- brutal honesty- but not in an abusive tone. Honesty covers a broad spectrum. Be honest about your emotions, your feelings, your body, your mind, habits, your things, your abilities, your skills. Be really honest. Don't fake them because the minute you fake something, it's going to catch up with you and you will be exposed. You'll be put in a situation to make a choice and then you'll feel compromised. You'll finally get tired of compromising because you've set unreal expectations, and were not honest. We need for you to be totally honest.

Loyalty

Reuben: A man needs a sense of loyalty from his woman. No matter what happens, he's got to know that she has his back and that she's going to be there for him. Nobody wants to be with a woman he can't trust, or feels as if he has to keep one eye on her and the other eye on the world. When the guy feels like his whole world is falling apart, that's when he wants to know that he can depend on his lady. He can trust her loyalty to him.

Marvin: The worst thing a woman can do to a man's pride, to insult him, is to befriend his enemy. To me, that is a lack of loyalty. It is sad to know that his woman can befriend a person who she knows does not like her man or accepts her man. If she doesn't have a good solid reason for not supporting him, such as abusiveness or cheating, she should have his back and keep his enemy at a distance. It's hard to reconcile how she can embrace his enemy as her friend, and for no good reason. He needs total loyalty from his woman.

To Be Loved

Robert B.: Guys like to be loved. They like to be able to say to others, "I have this woman and she will die for me." They need the power of being loved.

Gilbert: The man needs to be loved and understood.

Hooper: Sometimes a man needs to hear his woman say, "I love you."

Robert C.: A man might know that you like him and may even love him, however, they need for you to be more expressive. Some women hold back and want the man to do all the loving and saying, "I love you." If you love him, show it more, show him more! Be more expressive and say it more. Express your love to him more!

Good Communication

Gilbert: They need for their women to talk with them and not at them. Don't have your man under an inquisition. Some women do not talk to their man but they badger and question him and then wonder why he is so uptight and mad. They go on a witch-hunt and question the man on everything he does or did as opposed to having a conversation with him. Talk with him and do not talk at him, because when that happens, the woman has a tendency to talk down to the man as opposed to talking on the same level.

Ronald: He needs to be able to have a decent conversation with her.

Duncan: A man needs to be able to talk to his wife. He needs to communicate with her. He needs to be able to discuss the feeling of the relationship, which way or how well she feels the relationship is going. Communication is one of the key things that make a relationship work. A lack of communication may be a telling sign of why some relationships don't work.

Dominic: A man needs to be able to communicate with his wife. My wife and I check in with each other from time to time and ask- "Is everything alright? Am I where I'm supposed to be?" You have to make time to communicate with each other.

Gerry: A man needs for his woman to communicate. It's intimidating when she shuts down. If there is no communication, you don't know what the other person has resolved within themselves. You then start to spin wheels. You're just going through the motions until an opportunity presents itself to communicate. You don't know what that person is thinking because communication is not only vocal- but the body language stops, the facial expressions become blank. The words of endearment-- Honey, Baby, Sweetie, Sugar-- all slow down, e-mails aren't regular, calls during the day are infrequent, and your cell phone isn't going off as much.

Robert C.: You have to tell men what you want. Men know how to treat a lady but women need to tell them exactly what they want, how they want it. Talk to me and do not block me out. If I don't understand, make me understand. Once I understand, things will get better. If I don't know, there will always be something wrong. A man needs for his woman to communicate honestly.

Ryan: Both men and women have a responsibility to communicate. They both have a responsibility to be there for each other, to take up the slack for each other. If one party is not communicating clearly, that can cause just as many problems as not communicating at all. If one party has a problem acting out anger, or controlling their temper, it can be just as much a problem as not dealing with things, or bottling things up. Regardless of the personality traits you are dealing with it, is extremely important to have good and clear communication with each other.

Pampering

Joseph: A brother needs to be held sometimes. He needs that sensitivity. We cry, too. A lot of women, in this millennium, in these times, don't know how to relate to that. They want a roughneck. No matter how rough we are, every now and then, we need to be pampered.

Gerald: It doesn't matter how macho we try to be, most of us are "mamma's boys." That's why we often try to find companions who have certain nurturing and pampering qualities that our mothers possessed. We even act like babies when we are sick. Encouragement, serious pampering, and nurturing, every now and then, are needs men have.

Aaron: A man is playful in a guy sense. He needs attention. He needs to be held, caressed, and touched. At times- we need a lot of pampering.

Kevin: A woman needs to understand and accept that just as she likes to get manicures, pedicures, massages, and facials, a man should be able to do the same without being afraid of being thought of as gay. If that man does not feel good about himself, he's not going to be good to you. If you don't allow him to love himself, just as you expect to love yourself, he won't love you properly. When his confidence is up, he'll be a good man to you. When he feels good about himself, along with your support and encouragement, he'll be a better man to you. You should want your man to look good, sometimes at your expense. Not all the time, but sometimes say- "Here, honey, here's $200. Go and do yourself some good." Just like a woman loves it when her man comes into the house and gives her money, the woman should do her man the same way. Show your interest in your man. If he is really the one you want to be with, prove it by expressing it. Every once and a while, seriously pamper him!

Intimacy

Michael L.: Regardless of the house you live in, the presents you get, or the money you make, at the end of the day, every man wants to know that when he is spoken to- when his woman is speaking to him, listening to him, kissing him, or making love to him, that an intimate connection is being made. People spend their whole life to capture that type of intimacy. I's their whole quest. I think it is a simple quest, an adequate quest, and, if you can establish that, I think a really strong relationship and marriage can develop. A man needs that type of intimacy from his wife. Without that, things start to become undone. If you don't have intimacy in your relationship, just think what people will do. They could become restless. They may drink or gamble. In a lot of cases, infidelity occurs. They might do all those things just to fill or satisfy the void caused by "unwant" and the lack of intimacy. Men crave intimacy with their wives.

Down Time

Aaron: He needs a downtime when he comes home before he can be a daddy or husband. He needs his space and time to unwind.

Male Bonding

Mamy: Men need to be able to associate with other men. Women don't understand that need and sometimes that causes them to become suspicious of a group of men hanging out together. They feel as if they must be up to no good. They feel that they may entice your man to do the wrong thing. They don't realize they need that time together just like she needs her time with her women friends.

Jermaine H.: I need my space. Sometimes, as men, we feel like we need our space. Women don't always understand that. It's not that we don't want to be with you but we need the time and outlet to be with the guys, or have time for ourselves. I need my space with the guys. When you hang out with women, you have to act a certain way and respect the presence of the female. You can't really cut-up and do the things that guys like to do.

Robert C.: Men have to hang out with their

buddies. If you take that away from us, we will go insane. We have to have our home-boys. Your buddies keep you from being emotionally stressed. They calm you down and balance you out. A lot of women don't understand that men need that. You always hear, "Why do you have to go with him-- why can't we do that together?" Do not try to supplement one for the other. If I like doing a certain thing with my buddies, don't try to do it with me. It won't work. It's not the same. It will repel me instead of attract me to you.

Patrick: Women seem to want to be all encompassing in the daily life of a man. The man needs to go out with the guys from time to time. He needs to socialize. He needs that bonding with his male peers. Women don't seem to understand that. They take it as a transgression against them. It has nothing to do with them. They just need time to bond with their peers. They need time outside of the marriage. Women perceive that as the man not needing her in their lives as much as they once did, so they take it the wrong way.

To Be Respected

Daryl: A man needs to feel like he has some kind of control, even if he is at a point where he's not totally walking in control. Allow him to have that feeling in a way that works for your situation. He needs to know that you respect his authority as the head of the household.

Travis: A man needs a sense of success inside his family. It's kind of like being the "King of the castle." You work and deal with the issues of the world all day and when you come home, whether to a wife, or a family, you need to have that feeling of being special or significant in the home. You need the feeling of being respected.

Robert B.: The average man, if he is honest, has a tremendous need to feel respected. The average man has a tremendous need to feel that his woman places him in control because he does not like to feel that he is less than his partner. He needs to feel that he is contributing significantly to the relationship and that she respects his contribution.

Scott: In order for a family to be strong, the man needs to feel like a man and be respected as the man. He has to have the assurance that he is the man. Sometimes, that doesn't happen because too many women have taken the role of being the provider, the leader, the father, and the mother in the household and when they meet someone and it's time to give that up, it's hard because fulfilling those roles has become second nature to them. It's like, if you are used to getting up at six o'clock every morning, after a few years, whether the alarm clock goes off or not, you will wake up because your body is programmed to wake up at that time. In the same way, the female is so used to doing all the work, as the father, mother, and provider, that it becomes very difficult for her to relinquish that position to someone else, even if she really wants to. She has to relinquish control and give him the respect he needs to get the job done.

His Woman to Keep Him Strong

Rick W.: A man needs for his woman to help him stay strong. If a woman is trying to make you weak, she doesn't really care about you. In your weakest moments, you need that woman to be there. No matter what is going on around him he can count on her being there to help build him up, then he'll have no problem figuring out where he needs to be when times get rough. He won't have to go out drinking, chasing women, or hanging out with his buddies. He reasons, "I don't need anything else to make me weaker. I'm going where I can get strong-home to my lady!"

"And rejoice with the wife of your youth, as a loving deer and a graceful doe. Let her breasts satisfy you at all times and always be enraptured with her love."
Proverbs 5:18--19

Thirteen: Sensuality and Sexuality

Many married couples need to recapture the excitement, passion, and romance of their early days. I'm concerned that the busyness of their schedules, brought on by the diversity of their roles; husband/father, wife/mother, employer/employee, mentor/counselor, big brother/big sister, etc., has not allowed the relationship the time or attention it needs to keep it alive and thriving! I am even more concerned that the sexual act between many married couples has become no more than an occasional nighttime attempt to rid one's self of the stress and tension of the day.

Married couples, please consider the insightful manner in which the men distinguish sensuality from sexuality. I am most confident their sensitivity and insights will cause you to rekindle the fire and stimulate passions that will heighten true intimacy and bring new pleasures and true gratification to your love relationship ***and marital bed!***

How do you distinguish sensuality from sexuality?

Lawrence: Society builds on sexuality but sensuality is more than those stipulations. It's not what the media projects. Sensuality is being in tune to her natural desires which are: to be loved, respected, cared for, and nurtured. Sensuality is nurturing her natural desires.

Kevin: Make yourself appealing to your man because others will. You don't have to compete but you do have to do your part in keeping him satisfied and interested. There should be some playing and foreplay. After all, a plane doesn't just take-off. It has to have a runway. Your foreplay is the runway and your moment is when you're airborne!

Chau: Sensuality is sharing a deep sensitivity with your woman. It is being sensitive to her wants, needs, and desires. It's sharing physical and emotional tenderness with her.

Sylvester: Sensuality is giving a look to your mate that just makes their day. It's about being so much into each other that just being together makes everything feel so right and seem so perfect.

Gerald: Sensuality, within a relationship, allows you to be able to draw strength from the other person when you are weak. Sometimes, it's just by a touch. Therefore, when you seem to be getting outside of yourself- just a simple stroke or touch of that person re-energizes you. You two are one and have become so much a part of one another that touching that person reconnects you. The love and strength that you have deposited in them-- along with the love and strength they have for you-- ignites, and the both of you are recharged and energized!

Dominic: Sensuality can be a look, a smell, even a phone call. Sensuality is the flirtyness that causes that chemistry. It's being spontaneous, like sending flowers to the job, cooking dinner together, doing those little things. You see your wife doing things all the time and you just want to say "Go ahead and take a break- I got it." It's doing the little things you know pleases the other.

Joe: The holding hands, the kissing in the morning, the pet names. Sensuality is the touchy-feely kind of things.

Joseph: The difference is romance. Sensuality is romance; the dim lights, walks in the park, poetry, holding hands, incense, the oils, and the massages.

Roosevelt: A lot of men like to be touched in the right places- that special touch-- the way you place your hand upon the body and the way you kiss. A lot of women don't know that men need that. They want to be pleased just like you do. They need affection too. Men like bubble baths and candles. It makes him feel special. Sensuality makes men feel special.

Kleinberg: Sensuality is the emotional aspect of sexuality. The kinder you are outside of the bedroom, the more tender and supportive you are, the more physical or sexual your partner would want to be with you. Sensuality is doing the dishes with your spouse.

David: Sensuality is an art that arouses the senses in such a manner that even the way she brushes her hair can trigger an emotion in you that drives you to feel a closer attachment to her. Sensuality is how a person may flow or do a certain action that allows you to feel their spirit by your simple observance of it.

Malcolm: A woman can be standing off at a distance, if the light-- whether it is the sunlight, evening light or candlelight-- is right, there are certain ways that she can look at you and give off a glow- a glow to where-- it's hard to explain but you can behold her and be amazed! It's a weakening effect on the man if he catches it at the right time. It makes a man weak. It might be her hair, the way she stands, the way she positions her head, or maybe the way she is walking at the moment. She can give off the most sensual aura. Also, the way she touches you-- her initial touch lets you know just how sensual she can be.

Carroll: A sensuous woman is a woman who bears her soul. I find that very sensuous. The eyes are the gateway to the heart or soul, so I think a woman's glance can be sensual without being sexual. There are some glances that make you weak in the knees. Sensuality, to me, is more emotionally based as opposed to the physical.

Ty: Sensuality is doing things to keep the sexual relationship stimulating and exciting. If you have to get a book, get one. I'm not talking about being freaky or down- right raunchy, but you can do things or learn to do things that keep the sex alive and thrilling.

Duane: Sensuality is bringing spice into the marriage by doing things to arouse your mate. It's making sure that the home fires are kindled.

Tony F.: Sexuality is the lust, the immediate physical gratification. Sensuality is the spirit-driven love and passion. One is almost instant and the other is more lasting. Sensuality tends to be the underlying love, need, and desire. Sensual women deal with internal gratification, not only external gratification.

Julian: Sensuality is more of the aura you possess as far as the touch, the closeness, the eye contact, the flirtatious behavior. Whether it's playing with the hair or going grocery shopping. It's togetherness, the bubble baths, the candles, and the fragrances. Sensuality is foreplay. Touching and hugging really turn women on. It's doing things to build up to the sexual act like exploring one another, touching one another, trying to find new sensations. Sensuality is needed for the arousal part. You need to feel sensual.

Travis: Sensuality is being able to attract and turn each other on. Even after you've been together for a while, you still want to look good for each other. She still wants to be sexy to him and he still wants to catch her eye. Sensuality wants to keep each other "number one", still. Sensuality is being free to initiate romance. In a true relationship, sensuality always precedes sexuality.

Gilbert: Sensuality is a state of mind, a perception. Sexuality is an act. Sensuality is the atmosphere, the setting, the mood. You can be romantic without being sexual. The ambiance, the candles, the welcoming into the home-- how my wife meets me at the door can be very sensuous. Sensuality should begin before you get to the bedroom. Call one another and be sensual over the phone to build up sensuality, then you'll be ready when you do get home because sensuality leads to sexuality. Touch your wife. Let her know that she is still desirable to you!

Timothy: Sensuality has more to do with attitude, demeanor, and the ability to respond. Sexuality deals with decisions of how you're going to physically express yourself with your partner. Sensuality is the joining of two minds, two spirits, the common goal, the mutual perspective about love, caring, providing, and sharing. Sensuality is the sense of loving a person without acting in a sexual way. Sensuality deals with the true essence of what love means.

Gerry: Sensuality is intimacy, lying on the couch, hugging, kissing, touching. Sex is born out of intimacy. You have to learn how to be able to feel each other over the phone, through your words, and through your presence in a room. Kissing is sensuous. Sensuality is her arms about my body, touching me in places that she knows brings pleasure, or hugging in a way that lets me know I'm wanted. It's seeking out each other's hands, touching each other, and the immediate embrace is not a withdrawal. Sensuality is physical acceptance, extending compliments, wooing and dating each other!

Kenneth: Sexuality is that nature that attracts you or turns you on. Sensuality is to be in tune with all of the sexual organs of which the greatest is the mind. It is being engaged in what your partner feels, or the special way they have when they move a certain way or do a certain thing. It's doing things to keep the juices flowing, so to speak. Sensuality is being physical in different places or areas of the home. The mind is such a potent sexual organ, so talking to each other can be sensual. One of the biggest turn-ons is what is said leading up to the sexual act. Sensuality is being in tune with your partner. It's having that need within yourself to please your partner. It's incorporating all of your senses, using your energies and channeling them so you are totally focused and concentrated on your partner.

Aaron: The intimacy of touching, walking through the park with her head on your shoulder, having good conversation as you're holding hands. Sensuality is- out of the blue- saying, "I love you. I need you." Reassuring each other of who you are in each other's lives and that you can't imagine life without them. Sensuality is the sentiment of breathing that person. You look forward to seeing that person. Going to their job in nothing but a trench coat, opening it up and saying to them, "I was just thinking about you. Can't wait to see you at home!" You're on a rhythm and you know each other. She pays attention to me. She knows what kind of shoes I like, she knows my style. When she gives me a gift, it is the right thing, the right size, the right color. She's in tune with me. Being sensual is being intimate on a one-on-one level. It's not sex, the penetration or intercourse. It's none of that. It is the touchy-feely type of things. It's having chemistry with a person. You just know them. Sex is often over rated. Don't get me wrong, it is a very beautiful thing if it is not exploited but it can undermine what true intimacy is, its whole essence. When it's their birthday, you get happy about the opportunity to celebrate them. Sensuality is walking around the house naked. It is reciprocated foreplay; the way I touch you and you touch me, the way I hold you and you hold me. If I kiss you slowly, kiss me slowly. Sensuality is not being in a hurry, not moving too fast, but savoring the moment and the pleasure!

"Put off your old nature which belongs to your former manner of life and is corrupt through deceitful lusts, and be renewed in the spirit of your minds."
Ephesians 4:22-23

Fourteen: Her Necessary Adjustments

The areas to be addressed in this chapter are sensitive areas and need to be addressed with objectivity and impartiality.

Therefore, I solicited the responses of men who had no hidden agenda or secret motive for what they had to say. Their only intent was that their responses would encourage women to become their personal best, in every area of their lives.

What adjustments do women need to make: to their appearance; the manner in which they relate to one another; and to their personal selves?

Dress and Appearance

James: Moderation has always worked for me. Whether it is in dress or speech, it's just moderation. Not being faddish but setting a standard and then building upon that standard. It's setting standards for you in spite

133

of what society is doing. You need to comprehend that there is always a higher standard because fashion today may not be fashion tomorrow, but goodness lasts an eternity.

Carroll: Society has not been kind to women as far as putting so much pressure on their appearance. I think there is so much pressure on women to always be aware or cognizant of their outward appearance. I saw a woman who was putting on make-up while she was driving. I don't mind a woman tres' naturel- without all the stuff. I don't mind the emphasis on hair, make-up, etc. I just think it gets in the way of who she really is.

Ryan: I wish women would dress more for themselves and to feel comfortable in what they put on. To me, the sexiest thing in the world is confidence. A less attractive woman can be more attractive because they are in something that they feel comfortable in, and are confident and comfortable in being themselves. They are not trying to wear something that everybody else wants to see them in.

Chau: Not only do a lot of women compete with men but they also compete with other women. When they go out, they dress more for other women and to impress others. They need to just be themselves and stop trying to be someone they're not.

Sylvester: It's a plus when a woman looks good, but she should find out what her man likes. A lot of guys don't like makeup and fake fingernails. They figure that eventually it has to come off, so why not show them the real you? They would rather see the real you than that camouflage thing you put on.

Mark: A woman can be very deceptive, from her false nails, extensions in her hair, the bustier, the makeup, down to the high heels. They often don't give out the real image of themselves but they expect men to be honest when they're deceiving them from square one with their appearance. When you first meet somebody, you're not meeting them, you're meeting who they would like to be, or who they think you would like for them to be. After a while, you find out who they really are. You get home and find out that most of her wasn't real.

Kevin: Some men can't just look at a woman without imaginations exploding all over the place. So, women should keep themselves to the point where men would want to pursue you-- but not fleshly-wise or body wise. All you'll get out of the relationship is flesh and body. You won't get heart and soul. Flesh and body wears out. Mind and soul lasts forever.

Malcolm: Some women dress as if they are trying to be noticed. I mean, women's clothes are sharp- but some things they know they shouldn't even try to wear. Your clothes shouldn't be tight as paint. If your body's not for it, don't squeeze it up in it. That is not sexy.

Hooper: A man looks at the way you are, the way you carry yourself, and the way you dress, and says to himself that he wants you. Why? You're telling him how good you are by the way you dress, therefore, you attract him that way. If you dress conservatively, a man would have to look twice and understand that there is something unique about this woman. He'll think twice before he approaches you in the wrong way.

Duncan: In my mind, dressing provocatively may look nice- but it is a turn-off as far as somebody I would want to try to get more familiar with, or try to get to know more. You don't have to dress too conservatively but you should look nice. You don't have to try to show a lot of skin. Your dress could be a sign that you are someone a man would like to know a little more about, or get to know better.

Duane: A lot of women have very low self-esteem. Most men say that they can tell how a woman is by the way she dresses. It lets them know whether they want to go after her or not. If they're looking for a purely sexual relationship, he'll go after the one who walks around with the halter top, real tight shorts, showing a lot of cleavage, a lot of body, because he looks at her as an easy conquest.

Gilbert: Women should dress in a way that will not cause someone to make a remark that is degrading. In fact, their dress should be complimentary to themselves and their mate.

Gregory: Women should dress to be attractive but not to be flirtatious and unbecoming. The attire of women today doesn't leave anything to the imagination. They show you literally everything. They don't give men anything to long for because they show it all up front. Everything is so thin and so tight that you don't have to imagine about anything. It's frivolous when you put a lot of stuff "on" and don't put anything "in".

Travis: I think that a lot of young girls are dressing like women. It's unfortunate because a lot of men can't tell or don't want to tell the difference. Some young girls lie about their age and do not let men know that they're very young. It is very admirable when a woman can dress professionally, yet provocatively. It reveals her sensuality. Some women are so extreme in their dress until it becomes pornographic. I don't know if it is because of a low self-esteem, a style, or they are just trying to be accepted. Men may look and lust- but they will not be taking her home to meet mother.

Christopher: I will see a woman who has on very provocative clothing, I will look at her and I might desire her, but that's all. She will not come home with me and she will not meet my mother. Because men are looking at that presentation, it is hard for them to see other qualities that she may possess. She may be intelligent, an outstanding mother figure, but because we see her as a sex object first, it's hard to see her as anything else.

Rueben: As far as dress, women have to be careful of the inferences they give. You have to know the signals you send off. Truth is- a woman should be able to walk down the street in a thong bikini or a see-through top and not be bothered, but she has to understand the realities of what she does. Okay, she can say all she wants that she should be able to wear what she wants to wear, however, it's what she chooses to wear that leads men, women, and everyone to make a call on who they think she is.

Gerry: Women should dress to feel alluring, sexy, and attractive, but only for their man. She shouldn't do that for everybody on the street because some men just don't know how to register you, how to read you. They take it as an opportunity to sexualize you and not see you as an individual.

Robert C.: As far as dress-- you know what you need to wear. Don't put on things and then say- "Why are they staring at me?" I know that you are wearing it for yourself, but you know that people around you are going to look. If you see someone staring, don't catch an attitude or say anything to them, after all, you know what you're wearing and why you're wearing it.

Relating to One Another

Kleinberg: Not to sound too chauvinistic, but I like to see a return to the more traditional role. Women look down on women who are homemakers. That has got to go. There needs to be respect between women. A woman who is a "stay-at-home mom" needs to feel good about her role. Be proud to be a homemaker with family values.

Reuben: It's been my experience that women are even competitive with friends and relatives. It always seems to be an unwritten competition between women. They try to be better than the other woman, or try to exhibit something that the other woman doesn't have. Women can be friends and still be in competition. They talk out of both sides of their mouths. True friendship should be unconditional- not okay one day but not okay the next.

Robert C.: Women need to learn to get along with other women. Sometimes they don't because of the way another woman looks. Their lack of self- esteem tells them that they have to outdo her. For instance- "If she buys this, I'll buy that. If she gets her hair and nails done every Thursday, I'll get mine done every Wednesday." There's no need for that. Get in touch with yourself, and then you won't have these feelings when you come around other women.

Ryan: In my experience, women can be way too judgmental towards each other. They are sort of on the lookout for things to pick on, to judge about. I wish women would accept each other better. There seems to be a weird competitiveness among women. It is unfortunate how women seem to go through friends, or have arguments with friends because of pettiness.

Robert B.: If women say that they don't want to deal with jive men and nobody deals with jive men- guess what? There'll be less jive men. If women say- "I don't want a man who is not intelligent, not well read, or who is not about anything."- there will be fewer men who aren't about anything. Women don't truly understand the power that they have working as a sisterhood. Maybe it's because sisterhood does not always exist. Where it does exist, you have more accountability. You will have more accountable men when you have women who are accountable to each other. They would realize that the sisters are unified and wouldn't try to get over on another sister when they couldn't get over on the first one. True sisterhood would all have the same standards and expectations.

Personal Adjustments:
Don't Be Too Easy

Duane: Some women can be a little too revealing and trusting. Someone may have just come into their lives but within a week they have totally opened up to that person. They open up too quickly and easily, at times.

Michael B.: Women shouldn't give themselves away so easily. When they do, they allow the "dog" men to continue to act like dogs.

Joseph: Many women are too gullible and fall for the games some men play. They allow themselves to be easily drawn into their mischief.

Rueben: Some women are too rough around the edges. They need to learn that every man who makes them happy, they don't have to turn their feet up to. They shouldn't be that easy.

Aaron: Don't be so easily persuaded. Don't do things because someone expects you to do them. Do them because you want to do them.

Be a Parent

Rueben: I've seen women in their thirties who had children when they were in their late teens or early twenties, walk into a club and their child walked in right behind them. They get so embarrassed. Some women say that they want the best for their daughters, yet they seem to dress better and look better than them. You wonder how they could look like "this" and their daughters look like "that". It's obvious they don't take much time with their daughters to keep them on the same level as they are.

Gregory: Many women are trying to be more of a friend than a parent to their children. It's causing a lot of problems with children in terms of them not knowing who they are, where they are, or where they should be. Mothers and daughters are hanging out together, smoking and drinking together, being more like friends than mothers and daughters.

Lennie: A lot of women today aren't in the home taking care of their primary responsibility, namely the children. It is a real shame when children call grandmother "Mom" as opposed to calling their mother "Mom." That tells me that this woman is not spending time with the child. the child does not recognize her maternity, or as the one who is raising him, but as one who just pushed him out of the womb. That's sad.

Tony F.: Some moms really scrutinize their daughters. They want their daughters to carry themselves in a certain manner. If the child veers outside of that, then there's redirection and things of that sort. She tries to make her daughter fit the image she feels that she should project, and a lot of times, it is the image of an extension of her; meaning that some women are very determined to make their daughters become what they wanted to become, or live the life they may have abandoned or had to abandon, because of things that came into their lives unexpectedly. Mom to sons-- I've been around females who have held their sons responsible for the actions of their fathers. In some cases, they hold the child so close to them that the child doesn't get a chance to be just that-- a child. The young boy is cuddled and sometimes ends up being the daughter they wished they had. That is hard to watch. Also, I see the struggle with young men to own up to their responsibilities because mom is always there to bail them out, to defend them.

Be More Careful

Timothy: I don't think that a lot of young women realize how dangerous it can get out there. For instance, I know females who go out drinking with guys. They don't know how dangerous that can be. She doesn't realize that she can end up naked, in the backseat of a car, and never know how she got there. Women sometimes put themselves in situations where their health or safety is jeopardized.

Stop Male Bashing

Gregory: Women need to stop indoctrinating young women with- "There are no good men out there." In society, you have music videos and entertainers portraying the roughnecks. Everyone wants to wear rags on the head, shirttails hanging out, pants hanging down, and teenage females are doing the same thing. You have the roughneck females going after the pretty little girls and many of them-- out of fear-- are buying into lesbianism.

Have More Self Respect

Gerry: What upsets me more than anything is what women have allowed to be said about themselves by themselves. You take the music that's out there now. The women don't sing about relationships, love, devotion, or togetherness. It's about break-ups, take your stuff and hit the door, split, give me your money and I'll let you look at it, buy me a house and I'll let you touch it. It's ridiculous! It's not so much what they have on, it's what they are allowing to be said about themselves.

Gilbert: I am thinking about some of the videos. They're making money, but their esteem can't be high because of the way they are portrayed in the videos. In the videos I see, they're just a body-- no brains-- just a body. They need to change the image they are allowing the media to put forth. Even if they aren't like that, what the world sees is what the world believes. Women do not have to speak like they're from Yale, but they should at least speak with common sense. Delete the "Yo's," delete the Ebonics. It's okay in some settings but it isn't appropriate in all situations.

Aaron: Don't disrespect yourself. Don't allow men to call you out of your name, like "b's" or "ho's.

Duane: Women need to have love and respect for themselves. If you want people to love and respect you, you have to exhibit behaviors that demand respect or the qualities that will warrant respect. Seek God. Don't let peer pressure affect you. Peer pressure is so strong and prevalent in society today- "If so-and-so is doing that then I need to do it." Be an original. Don't accept the status quo. Do what you want to do and not what someone else is doing. For every action there is a reaction. You have to think about the consequences of everything that you do. Is it positive or negative? What impact will it have on you in the future? Think before you react. Stand on your morals. You are original and unique. No one can take it away from you unless you allow him to. Be yourself and don't let anyone force you or pressure you to do anything that you do not want to do. Respect yourself.

Be Yourselves

Kenneth: Stop fronting with facades, fake personalities, and lies about who you are or what you have. It's hard keeping that up. If you do, look at all the energy you are expending fronting a lie. You're better off being yourself. Whoever you attract should be attracted to you because you are yourself, and whoever loves you should love you for yourself. The more you get in touch with yourself, the more you know what you need or what you want. You'll recognize it when you see it. If you're not in touch with yourself, you won't know what you're looking for and you will end up with anything.

Rick W.: Women sometimes use themselves as a vessel or vice to get where they want to go. They do that in different ways; with verbal manipulation and deception. It's almost like putting a worm on a hook to catch the fish. They use different lures to catch the man. If this doesn't work, they try something else. Women should realize that being honest, sweet, and real is what intrigues and captivates a man. Most men are attracted to that more than the sex thing. When you reach a man mentally and spiritually, he'll physically try to take the relationship all the way!

James: I think it is very important to know yourself, to recognize your own shortcomings, and be willing to expose those things. When we hide certain things and keep them away from the relationship, we're coming to the table with a hidden hand. Those things have a way of coming back at the most inopportune time to taint what's already on the table, and then you have to do some patchwork. Once the damage is done, it's done. So it's better to be yourself upfront.

Nayoti: Women, be you. Don't put on a show. Be straight up and let the other person know what they are getting. The initial start is often a show. Later, you find out that they're nothing like they appeared to be in the beginning. That sets you back. It's like wasting a lot of time.

David: I'd like to see her be herself and be true to herself. She can then be true to you because she knows who she is. She won't have an identity crisis and won't be holding on to the baggage of how she is supposed to be based upon how someone else wants her to live. That's what triggers baggage sometimes. They're trying to live up to some imposed standard set by others.

Stop Playing Games

Ronald: Some women play games. It's like, who can they get over on?

Nayoti: Yeah, it's like, what can I get out of him?

Darin: I know that men do it, but some women have taken it to a whole new level. Men will play games for sex but women play games for material things. It's like-"If you buy me something, you can have pretty much what you want." But the gifts have to keep on flowing. As soon as they stop, the relationship is over. So, the relationship was based on me giving you money and me getting the sex, or me having you as a girlfriend- as long as I'm doing for you materially.

Michael R.: Be for real. Some women stack men up like you stack up cards. They'll get several men interested and then stack them up to see who the best is. They keep you hanging on and women should not do that. You're wasting a man's time. This guy could be going somewhere else. A guy has a lot at stake when he tells a woman that he likes her. A woman can make him feel like nothing and throw him off, or accept it. Just be real and head to where you want to be. Women, stop playing games to save face. Make smart decisions. Know what you want, what you're looking for. A lot of good guys will leave themselves out of a relationship purposely, or be by themselves because of dealing with stupid stuff and playing games.

Robert B.: Some women are players. They're not serious about being in a relationship. They aren't looking for a commitment. They want what you have and not what you are, unless who you are happens to be power, position, or fame. There are females who take life as a big game. Some aren't looking into your soul. They are looking for your pockets. She's not trying to see how good your spirit or character is- she's finding out how deep your pockets are.

Stop Using Children

Nayoti: A lot of women use children to tie down a man. They may really be interested in a particular man, but rather than making a commitment and trying to strengthen the relationship to possibly take it to marriage, they think if they have a child by him, then he'll always be in their lives. To bring children into a life situation for their own desires is wrong. Don't bring them into a world of confusion for your own selfish gain.

Ronald: Stop playing games with the kids when you've broken up, he has moved on, and you find out that he is with another woman. She now wants to keep the kids from him and she starts to play games. If he was a good father before he got involved with someone else, he is still a good father after he has someone new.

Christopher: Men do not bear children but we really do have good advice and parenting skills, therefore, we need to be given a chance to raise our children. Some women completely take over and don't allow the man to share in that responsibility, especially if she doesn't like his new woman.

Robert C.: Women with kids- do not push your kids off on me because they don't have a father figure. If I like kids, and come to meet yours, we will have a ball while I'm in their presence- but they are not my kids! Don't call me to say- "So and so is acting up."- when I only saw the kid twice! Do not push your kids on me.

Melvin: You can't pick and choose when I should be daddy. When it comes time to pay money, buy things, or when you want to not be bothered with the children, it's okay for me to be daddy. But when I'm trying to be proactive in raising the kids, and I detect a problem and try to tell you about it, you say that I'm trying to run your life. You need to let a father be a father.

Learn to Be Happy

Bill: I wish women could be happy with what God gave them. We all aren't going to have the perfect nose. Some of us are going to wrinkle faster than others. Some of us are going to have a couple extra pounds. I wish women were happy with their inner selves so that they don't have to dress provocatively, or act a certain way to be noticed. It's all about them being happy with themselves so that they aren't constantly trying to change something, somewhere; whether it's their make-up or the way they dress. But it's all on the surface for some women. They need to learn to be happy with themselves.

Be Motivated

Sylvester: I would like to see women have a little more gumption or get-up-and-go about themselves. Some of them tend to lay back and tell themselves- "This is it. This is all I know and this is all that I can do." That's a wrong way of approaching anything in life. If you maintain that attitude, you're not going to accomplish anything. You'll just sit still and hope for things to happen. Things just don't happen. If you want anything in life, you have to go and get it. You need the initiative to get up and do it. Stop telling yourself that you can't do this or you can't do that. When you do that, you are already defeated. You should feel as though you can accomplish anything you put your mind to. Trial and error. That's how you learn. That's how you get strong.

James: Women need to have an "in- spite-of" kind of determination. It doesn't matter where you start out at. It's how determined you are to make progress. It doesn't matter how incremental the progress is. The idea is to

make progress.
Be More Confident

Joseph: Women are seers. Most of the time, when you see things, your first instinct is normally the truth, but because they want love so badly, they become blinded by love instead of what they're actually seeing. Be confident and go with your first gut feeling. It's always the truth.

Greg: Some women need more confidence in themselves. They second-guess themselves a lot of times. The man is totally satisfied with who they are and how they look, but the problem comes when they look at skinny women walking up and down the runways and feel that they need to look like that. They watch TV and see how society says they should look, and then they want to look like that. The man doesn't want that. Being attractive is not all physical. It's what you say, what you do, and how you carry yourself. You can be physically attractive, yet totally unattractive.

Roosevelt: Women need to have more pride or confidence in themselves. When it's good confidence- it comes off in a positive way; you smile more, you're more pleasant, and you make better decisions. I think a lot of women have little confidence in themselves so they settle for less. They choose men who don't quite fit the bill and they start a relationship that's messed up already. They choose men who aren't really trying to accomplish anything for themselves. Because they don't have confidence in themselves, they will continue to go in a direction that will only breed more negativity. If they had more pride and confidence in themselves, they could present themselves in a way that will attract better situations.

Will: A lot of women should take the time to act with more confidence. They need to show up and have confidence. Women can act more timidly when they should take a stand. It seems like some women have bad things happen to them and keep allowing bad things to happen to them. They need to take a stand- to stand up for themselves and don't let people walk over them. If there is something you're not willing to do, be able to communicate that. Have more confidence in yourself, in what you want, and in what you will allow.

Set Higher Standards

Timothy: I would like to see women be more responsible for and about their actions. Maturity seems to be a problem for a lot of women. Maturity allows you to set certain standards that won't be compromised. If more women set standards and stuck to them, men would not get away with as much as they do.

Travis: I would make the point that women should set the standards. Men are willing to adjust to the standards of women. If a man is a scrub, don't deal with him. Let him know up front that you are not going to compromise what you want.

Robert B.: If women can come together and define the kinds of values and standards that they want in men, and agree that they're not going to deal with any man who doesn't meet those values or standards, guess what? Men would change. Women need to understand their own power. Once you define what you want in your world and who you want to be in it, you can control it. There are some sisters who get what they want because they have defined their world and exercise tremendous influence on the world they've defined. I know some women who do not allow themselves to become emotionally attached to certain types of men, even though they may like this person, because they don't want to marry this person, or they don't feel like this person will contribute to where they want to go. Women should take themselves as the most serious project of life. They need to be more real, and set higher standards. That would put them in a better situation to attract what they need to attract- and what God would have them to attract!

"A wise man will hear and increase learning and a man of understanding will attain wise counsel."
Proverbs 1:5

Fifteen: Addressing All Women

At the end of the interview sessions, I said to the men- "If you had the attention of all the women in the world, and were allotted 15 uninterrupted minutes to reveal what men wish women knew- what you would say?" **They said:**

Arnold: Always carry yourselves like ladies and dress accordingly. You'll get the attention you're seeking because you will stand out.

Chau: Be happy, be kind, be generous, be open-minded, but most importantly, be yourself!

Mamy: You are special. You have great ability and influence in the family. If you had a good upbringing, you have a good chance of becoming a positive and productive person in the community. Women, it was your positive influence in the home that produced positive citizens in society.

Larry: Give us some credit. We like that. Loosen up and try not to take everything so seriously. Number one point: speak up. I don't like the game playing and trying to figure out what's on your mind.

Joe: Don't sweat the small stuff along the way. Don't make a big deal out of small things concerning the relationship. The main important piece is that the man is willing to stick it out to the end and willing to take the relationship to its full potential.

Ryan: Don't take things so personally. You are not responsible for what a person thinks. Just because somebody says something and it feels personal, it may not have been directed towards you. What a person says, think, or does, is on them. It's in their heads. It has nothing to do with who you are. It's not about you. Even if it is- it's about what they perceive about you. It's about what is in *their* heads. Don't take things so personally. You can't carry that weight on your shoulders.

Michael B.: It's not that serious! Move on! Stop talking about it and just keep going! If he did something to you today, don't keep bringing it up tomorrow. If you resolved it or didn't resolve it, you can deal with it or you can move on. Move on! Stop griping about stupid stuff that happened or is happening. There are good guys out there who will do the right thing. You have to give them the chance. It's over, deal with it!

Leroy: Give a man the chance to show you who they are and then be accepting of who they are. What they do is a lot of their communication. Men are doers. Men communicate by their actions. Allow him to show you who he is or what he is about. Don't have pre-conceived notions about men as far as what they should do, or how they should act. Let them show themselves first and then you can judge them or draw conclusions.

Duncan: Give some time to understand a man. Go beyond the outward or surface. Look a little deeper. Don't judge a book by its cover. Don't just look at somebody and draw conclusions based on what you see externally. Go beyond the exterior. Give the individual a chance so you can learn what type of human being he is. You might learn that he is someone you like to learn a little more about, or you may learn that his interior is far superior to his exterior. If you dive into the individual, you may come to know his "person". You may learn a little more than what the exterior is telling you.

Christopher: Allow men to treat you like ladies. Allow men to protect and take care of you. Women do your best to resolve the issues with the parent of your child before you invite someone else in your life. You need to bring closure to that relationship. It should be a strictly cordial friendship, that's it. No creeping over there sometimes, or whatever. It needs to be ended before you bring someone else into your life.

Lawrence: Please know that when you have a man who knows what his position is and is providing it for the woman, once you realize that you have a man of God in your life, a man who is strong, who works, who is a builder, a provider, please realize that you have found everything you need in a man. You don't have to look elsewhere. Please realize that you have the perfect man for you.

Julian: All women have the capability of getting a man through sex. The task women have after the sex is how to keep the man. Keeping the man is really not that difficult. It's important to know what is important to him. Listen and pay attention to his interests, his likes, and definitely his dislikes. When he opens up, she has to be ready to take all that information and use it for good to help the relationship.

Gregory: Godly men want women to know that

they need somebody who can understand where they are from a spiritual standpoint, and who are willing to grow with them in a direction that is pleasing to God. You need someone who will enhance your efforts to be more like Christ, to be more pleasing to Him, so that you may grow properly and help others to grow, likewise. A man needs not to be put down or misled. So mean what you say and say what you mean. Be able to appreciate the man for who he is. Understand that a man has faults and he needs your assistance to help him work through them. I want to tell women to treat yourselves right and don't belittle yourselves. You are "Somebody." You are made for and with a purpose. Seek to be what God wants you to be. Take care of yourselves. Always look to God for strength and direction.

Gerry: The only way to love, trust, respect, and satisfy us emotionally, physically and mentally, because you really can't just do one aspect and have a balanced or fulfilling relationship, is to open yourself up spiritually and introduce him to spirituality.

Kenneth: Walk away with the idea that the most important and the most pleasurable things that we could ever do are heightened when that person is of the opposite sex, and are multiplied even more when you like that person as well as love that person. It is even greater when they are truly considerate of you, and feel it important enough to be conscious of making you happy. I would like women to understand that they have a lot of power. It is the creative power of giving and not withholding. It's positive energy and women should be more discriminating about who they give that gift to. A man should not earn that gift by anything that he does but by who he is.

Joseph: I want to say to the women- don't be fools

for love. You may think you love a person but sometimes it's not love, it is a habit. We do things out of habit. Evaluate the whole situation so that you won't get caught up in something that it's not. You're searching for something that you really have to find within yourself, which is love.

Mark: The measure of a man is not in his wallet but his character. Men, as well as women, need help to be the person they envision themselves to be. That's why people get together. I would want to be with someone who could help me become the person I envision myself being. But we don't do that. We try to find our perfect mate, the perfect person, and they're not there. You just have to work with each other and help each other to become the person- not the person you want him to be- but the person he wants to be. Don't get with someone to make him who you want him to be. It won't work out.

Hooper: Get yourself together with God. If you really want to seek someone, seek Him. I guarantee you that your life will never be the same. Also, when someone tells you that you're no good and that you will never be anything, you'll never make it, make a determination to prove to that person that they are wrong and that you are "Somebody". Know that when a woman does not respect herself, she has already lost the battle. Let God give you a man. Stop trying to go out there and take all the men that you know are not good for you.

Bill: Love yourself. Do not define yourself by what men, other women, or society thinks. Be true to yourselves. Make sure you do what you think is right in your heart and not what other people think is right. Treat the people in your life the way you would like to be treated and don't differentiate that or don't change that. Understand that every person on the planet, especially in

2015, goes through struggles. Love yourselves. Make sure you fulfill what you think will make you happy. Unfortunately, people think that making yourself happy is a selfish act. But if you are happy, others around you will be happy. Take that time to take a dance class for an hour a week. Don't be afraid to go to Zumba classes or to the gym. Don't feel guilty because you are a mother or wife and you want to take the time to do something personal for yourself. Stay true to yourself. Don't constantly try to fit the mold or ideals of others. Remain true to who you are.

Rodney: Women were made for men according to the Scriptures. Men need women. You are very vital to society. You were placed here to be beside a man and not behind him. Women need to hear that men and women need to co-exist, because men really need women.

Timothy: We love you! We need you! We need you to know that you are needed and loved. We need you to take every ounce of your being to uplift yourself, to empower yourself. Take that time to find your greatness. Find the history of your greatness. Get in touch with it and use it. Understand that you were created to be at the right hand of man. You are everything to us. We're nothing without you.

David: Listen, love, and be loved. If you don't listen, you can't love and won't receive love. You need to understand that your man is not your child. Don't build these walls based on past experiences. Have standards but let your standards be reasonable. Put prayer into your relationship. Have an understanding of what you want so that you can communicate that, and won't have a relationship based solely on sex. You could find yourself in a relationship for 18 years, never married, have several children, but you're stuck in a relationship where there is no real love. Pray about your relationship and let God send you a good man. Don't be afraid to be honest with others, and most definitely yourself. If he is not what you want, move on. Don't be miserable or unhappy.

Aaron: Before you judge me, know my heart and know it well. What men have to give is powerful. You can trust it and you can believe it. A real man's word is his bond. If he says it, he will do it. He will shield you and protect you. Trust him if he has invested time and energy in you. If he says he loves you, believe him. Believe that he loves you and that you are deserving and worthy of his love.

Will: If I could pound home one thing, it would be the concept of communication. Take the time to get to really know a person before you fully commit and take the bigger steps; becoming his girlfriend, becoming his wife. I think there are so many failed marriages because too many people acted before fully surveying the scene, so to speak. There are so many people out there, and if you took the time to look into their lives, you will be surprised of what you can learn from them; what they like, what they don't like, what they like about you, what they don't like about you. If more people actually took the time to really get to know someone before jumping into a relationship right away, you won't see so many relationships start and end. So many people backslide and flip flop back to each other. Why would you go back to that person? Why did the relationship end? Did you really consider whether that person will change? Does he have to change? Is he going to change? Should he have to change? Should you consider looking at someone else? You may have been close at one time, but, you two didn't meet the mark. Be patient and take the time to survey the person. Take a look into their life and see how your life matches with theirs.

Tony F.: There are real men in the world. All men are not obsessed with sex. Sexuality and desire is part of life, but I like for women to understand that there are good guys out there but you treat them like crap, particularly when they're young. There are ones out there who just want to go through as many women as possible. The ones who are selective and have the woman's interest at heart, you overlook them. You don't realize that they're the ones you end up marrying. There are men in society who are real, and they do what they are supposed to do for females, physically and spiritually. The saying, "Men are dogs" is dead. You attract the type of people in your life who truly echo your spirit. If you constantly get negative people around you, it may be because of the aura you give off. It may not be intentional, but ultimately, the kinds of people in your life, relationship-wise, are the kinds of people that you attract. As you enter into womanhood, you must ask yourself if the problem is those people who are in your life, or if the problem is you for letting them into your life. Also, your perception of the relationship may not be what your partner's perception is. If you never sit down and find out his perspective before you get into the relationship, you've surrendered the opportunity to make a wise choice. If you're too persistent about being in a relationship because you just can't be by yourself, you have to have a man, or you're so angry that you don't want to be in a relationship with a man, realize that you didn't lose a man, you lost yourself. Somewhere in that equation you lost who you are. Find you. Bring you to the table and don't bring every boyfriend you ever had to the table. Don't bring situations, bring experiences. Bring the desire to constantly understand self. The more you understand self and can articulate that- the easier the relationship will be.

No man wants to be around someone who is arguing within themselves. To enter into a relationship you have to not just see today or tomorrow-- you have to see forever. If you don't see forever with that person, why even hang around for a little while? Why temporary? Why not forever? Why would you even do that to yourself? You're just giving yourself a reason to be tortured. If it's not real, or if it's not right, it's wrong. Accept it for what it is. Women need to really ask themselves what they really want. Do I want money? Do I want love? Do I want companionship? What do I really want? Do I want temporary or forever? There's no more of that 50-year marriage thing happening- that's scary!

Robert B.: Women, stop seeking love and lovers, and become or be love. When you are love, you will attract love into your life. Become the person that you want to attract in your life. Be godly. The most important thing we can be in our lives is a perfect reflection of God. Being one with God and working at becoming one with God prepares you for life. We can become better people if we behave how Jesus Christ behaved. Try to walk in His footsteps. Try to model His behavior, *and,* if a man *never* comes into your life, that's cool- *He will give you a beautiful and fulfilled life!*

ABOUT THE AUTHOR

D. Jackson resides in Baltimore, Maryland and has been employed as an Educational Support Professional for the Baltimore Public School system for over 20 years.

D. Jackson attended Morgan State University, Baltimore, MD, majoring in Mental Health, and is a graduate of the Victory School of the Word, Philadelphia PA.

D. Jackson , Author/Publisher/Motivational Speaker, has written several books and curriculums for civic and religious organizations.

To order copies, go to:

Amazon.com
Barnesandnoble.com
Createspace Estore
deejackson7@comcast.net

For speaking engagements, book signings,
radio and television interviews, and other events,
please contact **D. Jackson** at:

Email: deejackson7@comcast.net
Phone: 443-414-4812.
Facebook: DeBorah Jackson